D1564127

The
Kitchen Sink
Papers

Other Books by Mike McGrady

Non-fiction

A DOVE IN VIETNAM

STRANGER THAN NAKED,
    OR HOW TO WRITE DIRTY BOOKS FOR FUN & PROFIT

Fiction

NAKED CAME THE STRANGER

The
Kitchen Sink
Papers

MY LIFE AS A HOUSEHUSBAND

MIKE McGRADY

DOUBLEDAY & COMPANY, INC.
Garden City, New York   *1975*

This is for *Siobhan*.
There are choices.

Library of Congress Cataloging in Publication Data
McGrady, Mike.
    The kitchen sink papers.

    1. McGrady, Mike. 2. Husbands. 3. Home economics—
Biography. I. Title.
HQ756.M23   301.42'7
ISBN 0-385-04879-3
Library of Congress Catalog Card Number 75-5263

Lines of poetry from *So . . . Help Me, Lord* by Alton H. Wilson. Copyright
© 1974 by Alton H. Wilson. Reprinted by permission of Doubleday & Company, Inc.

The
Kitchen Sink
Papers

ONE

I had it made.

At the age of forty I had been married for sixteen years to a woman of intelligence and beauty. The three children seemed to be growing up straight. My job—writing a newspaper column —brought prestige, an annual income of $35,000, a measure of artistic satisfaction. And that's not to mention the $70,000 home in a quiet suburb, the new swimming pool, two cars, and the rest of it.

I was a happy man who had been rewarded by life beyond even a mother's expectations, one of those rare individuals who feel good driving toward work in the morning, good again driving toward home in the evenings. I was always driving toward things, never away from them.

One day, late in 1973, with all my affairs in order, I quit my job and became a housewife.

* * *

Possibly that fact will cast doubt on the earlier description of my life. I would point out that the very harmony of my life was one of the reasons for changing it. Everything had been going too well, had gone too well for entirely too long, and as I passed still

1

another milestone birthday, I found myself wondering whether even paradise would turn out to be a colossal bore.

When life flows too smoothly, it passes without leaving a mark. I was doing one day what I had done the previous day, what, in all likelihood, I would be doing the coming day, and often I felt that I was on a train that was gathering momentum, that the increasingly familiar landscape was being reduced to a blur.

In most lives there is no way to slow down the machinery or to change the direction. To even contemplate such an act would have been scarcely possible were it not for a wife who had spent the past few years going through more than a few momentous changes in her own life.

Like many women who came of age in the 1950s and 1960s, Corinne had been charting a course toward liberation ever since our third child was out of diapers. Sensing that her freedom was connected to her ability to produce—and perhaps just weary of accepting a weekly allowance from a grumbling husband—Corinne had done all those things that women do to make pin money.

Working as a part-time poll taker, she became a familiar figure on our neighbors' door stoops. Several Christmas seasons were spent going from one gift store to another, selling hand-made tree ornaments. And a half-dozen years ago, working with a friend, she retreated to the basement and began pasting together plastic gee-gaws and baubles, constructing jewelry of a conspicuous gaudiness that had, in the era of Camp, found a warm welcome in some of Manhattan's most prestigious shops. Its success was its destruction; it inevitably inspired a host of imitaters, people with a surer knowledge of machinery and salesmanship and distribution and larceny.

Corinne went from jewelry to plastic furnishings—plastic because it was readily available and because it could be bent into any of a thousand shapes when placed for a minute over a simple hot wire. With equipment no more elaborate than that, she designed and manufactured magazine racks, tables, picture frames, recipe bins, napkin holders, and, most notably, a see-through cookbook stand that she had the foresight to patent.

She knew the cookbook stand would be a success. She knew this because everytime she sold it to a store, the store would send it to other plastic companies where it could be copied or, as the designers put it, "knocked off." Corinne would call up these thieves and shout at them and once she picketed them, but what stopped them finally was dragging them into court and suing them.

Gradually, her business grew. Just how much became clear to me one day late in 1973 when I visited her shared office above a candy store on the main street of town. This, incidentally, was no small thing. As another woman once explained to me: "Corinne is an inspiration to us all; she's the first woman to move up from the basement to an office—it's our goal." Corinne was on the phone when I came in the door.

"I'll have to check that out with my shipping department," she was saying. "I think the answer is yes, but if you can hold, I'll get the information at once."

"What's this?" I said. *"What* shipping department?"

"Later," she whispered.

There was no time for conversation. She rushed to the files, thumbed through several dozen folders, found the correct invoice, and sprinted back to the phone.

"I just checked with shipping," she said, "and your order went out two days ago. You should be getting it any day now."

I had known the chief executive officer of Corinne McGrady Designs for sixteen years and I knew her to be a preternaturally honest woman on all matters of substance. If she wanted to refer to a filing cabinet as a shipping department, well, that was her business. Then, a second telephone call.

This time: "Our salesmen are out of town now and we'll have to wait until they call back in." Okay, true enough, there were agents in several cities and that was surely allowable. Then, this: "But I can't promise delivery until the week after next—the trucks are all on the road now."

"Trucks? What trucks?"

"I didn't say *my* trucks," she explained. "I always say *the* trucks. And the fact that the trucks happen to belong to United Parcel didn't seem all that relevant at the moment. And if they're not on the road now, then UPS is in deep trouble."

The business was coming along. Only a few years earlier, back in the plastic-jewelry days, Corinne had done well enough to be noticed by the New York *Times,* where she was once described as a "housewife" and a second time as a "suburban housewife." As a result of this, her largest single account canceled out; it seems they were too professional to do business with a mere housewife.

When Corinne advanced this theory, I suggested she was being too sensitive, that the important thing—the only important thing—was that the name be spelled right. However, I took the trouble to read dozens of stories about businessmen and seldom read mention of their marriages and never once saw any of them referred to as a "suburban househusband."

Corinne learned, in the early days, that some companies were reluctant to pay their debts to a mere woman. In fact, this is how I became actively involved in the growing firm. On slow days at the office, I would pick up the telephone and read a small speech that I had typed out.

"Hello, this is Mr. Dempsey," I would lie. "I'm calling from the accounting department of Corinne McGrady Designs and we've noticed that you haven't paid your bill and we were wondering what are your plans in this regard."

Interestingly enough, the mythical Mr. Dempsey got paid a great deal more rapidly than the real-life Mrs. McGrady. And he enjoyed certain other advantages. For one thing, no one ever called him "sweetie" or "honey" or ever once said to him, "What's a cute thing like you doing in a big business like this?" Also, no one ever tried to proposition him over the phone or to suggest a late supper where they might discuss the matter to better . . . ah . . . advantage.

As recently as this very morning, I was on the phone reading from a second piece of paper.

"Hello, this is Mr. Young, purchasing agent for Corinne McGrady Designs. I'd like to speak to your sales department."

It has been our experience that a male voice can get through to a firm's sales department three times as often as a female voice.

Furthermore, we've learned that there are two prices for plastic. The one Corinne had been paying. And the other one, the lower one, the price she was able to get when she called up and introduced herself as "the secretary for Mr. Young, purchasing agent for Corinne McGrady Designs."

Well, despite everything, the corporation grew and prospered, and by late 1973 it seemed far removed from its beginning days,

4

the days when the only voice speaking for Corinne McGrady Designs might belong to a four-year-old child. "Mommy gone by-by," he would inform the buyer from Bloomingdale's.

So I learned to accept the mythical fleet of trucks on the road, the salesmen who were beating down doors throughout the civilized world, the shipping department that came disguised as a file cabinet. For what I saw, beyond all that, was one determined woman at work—and apparently that was something the rest of society was not quite so ready to accept.

The year that I decided to become a housewife, Corinne's income had risen to the $10,000 level for the first time. I must point out, however, that level of success had not been achieved overnight or without some shared sacrifice. During the previous several years, we had spent our weekends with the children in the basement, simultaneously violating the zoning ordinances and the child-labor laws, painstakingly bending sheets of clear plastic over homemade heating machines. I will reveal, with some pride, that at my peak I was able to singlehandedly turn out eight cookbook stands a minute.

In gaining a businessman, I had lost a housewife. What that meant, in effect: I had also lost a servant. Meals soon became haphazard affairs that forced the kids to get by on their wits and the previous night's leftovers. Once a week, a cleaning woman came in, sighed philosophically, and attacked the small mountain of debris that had accumulated in every room.

Although the situation took some getting used to, it was not without its brighter side. I was delighted to discover that children seem to survive best when ignored most. The moment we stopped straining to provide amusement for them, they learned to amuse themselves. When the three meals a day stopped appearing on the table magically, they learned how to cook. And when we stopped cleaning their rooms for them—well, thank God we had the cleaning woman.

It was not all sacrifice. Three years ago Corinne first started to show a profit and that went toward things the family might never otherwise have purchased. A camping trip across the country. An Eames chair. An Italian stereo set. Even a swimming pool. And by 1972 there was enough money coming in so that Corinne asked me to stop paying her a weekly allowance—the $100 that went for food, help, and incidentals. Naturally, as I escaped some of the financial burden, Corinne sought to escape some of the housewifely burdens. Two nights a week, I assumed responsibility for feeding the family—what this meant, in practice, was that two nights a week we went to McDonald's or the local pizza parlor.

There was nothing unique about our experience; many of my male friends were learning the shortest route to McDonald's at the same time.

However, there was nothing in my personal history to adequately prepare me for the phenomenon known as women's liberation. I could appreciate the fact that I was gaining a happier, more fulfilled, more functional human being as a wife; still, I was not entirely sympathetic. Like other males, I did not fully understand the nature of the female complaint.

I would say: "I can't come home and cook dinner every night or even every other night. I've got a job to do. And my work takes too much out of me."

She would say: "You always forget that I go to work, too."

I would say: "But that's your own business and you can set your own hours—you could stop anytime you like . . ."

She would say: "But if I stop early, the business isn't going to succeed. And my business is just as serious to me as your business is to you."

And I would say: "But it's my job that pays all the bills. I can appreciate that you should be working, but someone still has to meet the month-by-month bills."

And she would say: "Well, let me contribute toward the bills and you do more around the house . . ."

And I would say: "Oh, no, I want you to put your profits back into your business. I don't want you spending your money on dumb things like bills. How's your business going to grow unless you put the profits back to work?"

And she would say: "How's the business going to grow if I can't spend any time at it?"

Secretly, I felt she was being unreasonable. Seen from the outside, her life seemed marvelously uncomplicated, free of stress and responsibility. She did not have to fight commuter traffic every day of her life, did not have to wage daily battle with executives who spent eight hours a day proving out the Peter Principle. Nor did she have to begin every new month by sitting down with a checkbook and scribbling away her savings. Although I kept these sentiments into the year 1973, I was smart enough to keep them to myself.

There were, however, aspects of her life that provoked unqualified envy on my part. All that free time. My life, on the other hand, seemed to be a scramble, a frantic search for a day to play golf, an evening to read a current book, a few minutes to get beyond the headline in the daily newspaper.

One lives alone in the pressure cooker. Our physical appearances told the story. As a result of that pressure—somewhere during all those three-martini lunches, those fifteen-cigar days, those expense-account working trips—I had accumulated forty extra pounds of unneeded weight, a blood-pressure count and a cholesterol reading that caused seasoned doctors to blink. The day I quit my job I weighed in at a plump, 235 pounds, and the gray hairs were arriving in multiples.

Corinne, on the other hand, like most of the wives in our circle of friends, had remained in fine fighting trim and, in fact, weighed five pounds less than she did on the day we were married. My own explanation for this: her life was relatively relaxed. She had a different explanation. Her argument was that men could let themselves go and no one cared; that I, for example, would be judged on the three columns I turned out every week, not on the two chins competing for available space above my collar. She pointed out, further, that although she was the president of a thriving small business, she was still more likely to be judged on the thrust of the breast or the slope of the belly.

At the time, I understood only a portion of what she was saying. In fact, I often thought how nice it would be if we could trade places.

I would say: "But now the kids are all in school—and you can do whatever you want. You can paint. You can read. You can go back to school. If you want, you can just take it easy."

She would say: "I've got plenty to do—I've got a business to run and a house to keep up."

I would say: "But you can get up when you want and go where you want and do what you want—I'd give anything to have that kind of freedom."

7

She would say: "You'd go crazy. You couldn't stand it. It'd be like being in prison all day. Without an office to go to, you'd . . ."

I would say: "I'd be happy if I never saw the inside of an office again."

And she would say: "You don't have to. You could stay home and be the housewife . . ."

And I would say: "Believe me, if we didn't need the money . . ."

And she would say: "We don't. I'm making enough to pay all the bills."

And I would say: "But if I became a housewife, you'd have to devote full time to your business. You'd have to go to the office every day and work eight hours . . . and, of course, I'd need an allowance. I'd have to buy all that food . . ."

And she would say: "How does a hundred a week strike you?"

And I would say: "I wish we could talk seriously about this."

And she would say: "Who's not being serious?"

TWO

The seed was planted but nothing came of it immediately. I stayed on the job, put on another pound or two, watched Corinne's business continue to grow, and occasionally sat through a replay of the original argument.

Corinne would make the offer—why didn't I stay home and take care of the children? I would threaten to accept the offer; she would threaten to accept my acceptance; I would warn her that I just might accept her acceptance of my acceptance. And after a few moments of bluff-and-parry, we would usually have the good sense to drop the discussion.

I had always told myself that I could quit the newspaper on a moment's notice. The quest for security is all too often the death of creativity and I had early decided to survive without security. If things failed to go my way at *Newsday*—why, I'd just pack it in.

At times that seemed to be an inevitability. I had issued more than my share of ultimatums. Either things—editing, office, as-

8

signment, travel, byline, salary, whatever—would go my way . . .
or else. Although I had survived a long string of these showdowns,
I was always aware that you only had to lose one.

But, as I told myself, that wouldn't matter. Which just goes to
show that you should never trust a man who talks to himself. The
truth of the matter was that somehow, through the passage of
time, I had become afraid of losing my job.

And whenever I contemplated leaving and trading lives with
Corinne, I found myself totaling and retotaling the blessings of the
job. I was finally in a position to submit my copy without having
to fear the heavy hand of the editor. The columns were being
carried to several hundred papers on the Los Angeles *Times* wire,
and an increasing number of papers was picking them up every
week. The salary showed no signs of leveling off. And there was
even some local celebrityhood—it was difficult to walk into any
saloon on Long Island without being recognized.

Moreover, I was becoming aware of age. I kept reading how
difficult it was for anyone past the age of forty to find work. After
a dozen years at the same paper, tenure had been built up and my
retirement pay—in just another quarter of a century—would
come to $1610 a month.

Retirement pay! At that point, the point when I started counting
my retirement pay, I knew it was time to leave. And think what it
would mean to Corinne—she would finally be free to see just what
she was able to do. I couldn't help but wonder what would happen
if she were able to go to an office and spend eight consecutive
hours conducting her business. How well could she do?

Interestingly enough, I had no *macho* qualms whatsoever about
her paying the bills. After sixteen years, I was more than ready for
a sabbatical from that particular chore.

I noticed another interesting phenomenon. Whenever I would
think seriously about leaving my job, whenever I stopped to examine my work objectively, much of it seemed meaningless.

The triviality at times proved overwhelming. Never more so
than when I would open my morning mail—the regular releases
from the American Optometric Association, the notice of the arrival of a brand-new starlet-author, the crayoned threats from my
more perturbed readers, and once every year a telegram:

9

"YOU ARE CORDIALLY INVITED TO MEET THIRTY OF THE MOST
BEAUTIFUL WOMEN IN THE WORLD AT A COCKTAIL PARTY FOR
THE MISS UNIVERSE BEAUTY CONTESTANTS FROM EUROPE, THE
MIDDLE EAST AND ASIA."

I don't think the phrasing even changed from one year to the next. In order to renew my credentials in the fraternity of general-interest columnists, I had responded affirmatively to the invitation more than once in the past. But all that ever came from covering the event was a temporary disinterest in overly symmetrical eighteen-year-old girls.

Ever since the emergence of women's liberation, the beauty contest has become a déclassé institution, the final bastion of the male-chauvinist-pig mentality. And the columnist who dares cover such an event does so in the full realization that the next day's mail will be heavy with opprobrium.

But the telegram happened to arrive on a slow day. A slow day for a columnist is one during which, by noon, no politician has made a spectacle of himself, no new season has begun, no man has bitten dog.

And so, feeling just the slightest bit guilty, I found myself on a sub-roof of the New York Hilton, standing beside thirty well-rounded young women wearing day-glo bathing suits. The women were being besieged by photographers, reporters, and television cameramen, who asked them to do such things as smile, wave, and inhale. The women did these small tasks rather nicely, as it turned out, and the windows in the surrounding skyscrapers soon filled with applauding male office workers.

I took out my pencil and pad but could think of nothing to write down. Nor could I even think of anything to ask the waiting beauties. So I eavesdropped on the other reporters, those who still had questions to ask. One of the contestants I listened to was Miss USA; she had won thirteen other beauty contests, including Miss Reno and Miss Washoe County and Miss Hawaii.

"Surely you take exception to all this," I said.

"To what?"

"To being treated like cattle." She seemed not to comprehend my meaning. "To being lined up here and examined like so many blue-ribbon heifers at a county fair."

"Listen," she snapped at me, "these beauty contests have paid my way all through college."

"What did you major in?" another reporter asked.

"Physical education," she said.

"And I'll bet you were an honors student," he said.

"Thank you," she said.

"Do you have a steady boy friend back home?"

"No," she said.

"Really?" he asked.

"Really," she said.

"No kidding?" a photographer asked.

"No kidding."

At this time another reporter joined the conversation.

"You're certainly tall," he said.

"Yes," she said.

"I notice that most of the girls here are tall," he said, pursuing the subject relentlessly. "Would you call that a trend?"

"Tall girls tend to look better in clothes than short girls," she said.

"Is that to imply," he pressed on, "that short girls, then, look better out of clothes?"

I drifted away then, not waiting for her response. Writing this kind of a column was becoming difficult—either I had written the same column sometime in the past or it was not worth considering a first time.

I don't know the exact moment when I decided to quit—but one reason was certainly that I had done the job long enough. Time was a key issue. After a dozen years, I had done the job as well and as poorly as I was apt to do it in the future.

And part of it was my love for the job. No longer did I easily tolerate those days when things fell apart, when I didn't do much more than fill the space. To stay longer was to risk the built-in hazards of the profession—to become repetitious and boring and predictable; or, to burn out. In recent years I had sought ever more frequent leaves of absence and ever longer vacations. Those were simply delaying tactics. It was time to try something new—and I had an offer, an intriguing job offer from my wife.

Actually, the offer had remained general in nature. Never once did we sit down and work out the specifics; at no time did we consider all the ramifications that a trade of roles would involve. The agreement was simplicity itself. I would do what she had been doing. She would do what I had been doing.

One day in November I arrived at the office, had my usual two cups of coffee, and typed out a two-paragraph letter of resignation to the editor, David Laventhol. The managing editor, Lou Schwartz, a longtime friend who shared my interest in horses who run around large ovals for prize money, stopped in that morning to inquire about the possible outcome of the day's feature race at Aqueduct.

"I've finally decided to quit," I told him.

"That's nice," he said. "What do you think of Windy's Daughter today? Do you think she's ready?"

"I'm serious, Lou." The trouble was that Lou had heard the speech before, and not just once. "I've written the letter."

"*Are* you being serious?" He saw that I was. "Well, I'd urge you not to go ahead with it. At least let's talk it over. There may be alternatives."

For once in my life, I was not looking for alternatives. In the past, the alternative offers had always been a source of great interest. A person cannot know his worth until he risks all. Those biggest salary increases always came the day I started to clean out my desk drawers. And the alternatives that came up now that I was again about to leave—wider syndication, diminished work demands, greater freedom of movement—were reassuring and would have been most welcome a month or a week earlier; but now it was too late for alternatives.

The memo of resignation contained two short paragraphs, just two simple thoughts. One, I had enjoyed the experience at the newspaper. Two, it was time to move on.

And then I went off to fill a luncheon obligation arranged weeks earlier. The meal was with an aluminum-siding magnate; a recent column on a governmental investigation of his operation had aroused his ire and he asked for the opportunity to present his side of the case.

He arrived at the restaurant driving a mauve Cadillac. Before we had made it from the cocktails to the baked clams, he told me how much money smart investors had made by getting in early.

12

He mentioned that he had been the first to be involved and had made more than he ever thought possible.

"Money's not everything in life." I coined that one on the spot. "Your customers are more worried about their aluminum siding than your profit—how about them?"

"Since when is money not everything?" he said, neatly ignoring my question. "If money's not everything, why do you get up and go off to work every morning? If it's not for the bread, why do you get dressed up in that monkey suit and slave away the day in the office . . ."

"Today you happen to be asking the wrong person," I said. "This morning I sent in a letter of resignation. I'm quitting the job."

"Yeah, and what're you gonna do for money now?"

"My wife's going to pay the bills for a while."

"Beautiful," he said. "What happened, she come into money?"

"She works—she's got her own business."

"And what're you gonna be doing while she's out chasing up the buck?"

"I haven't figured that one out yet," I said. "I'm figuring on doing what she does—I'll stay home and make sure the kids get fed and the house is clean and like that."

"You're putting me on."

"Nope."

"Well, you *oughtta* be putting me on," he said. "What kind of work is that for a man to do? I can't imagine any real man settling for a chickenshit life like that."

I had no response and it was just as well. After that, I don't think the aluminum-siding king heard a word that I said. He made a few perfunctory remarks about the column and then settled down to eating the meal as hastily as possible. It was quite clear that he had dismissed me. At the end of the meal he did say he hoped that I hadn't gotten the wrong impression—the real reason he was in business was not the profit, well, not the profit *exclusively,* but because aluminum siding was a good thing for mankind. And that's the kind of guy he was and, asamatterafact, he had just come back from a three-day religious retreat.

"And let me tell you what my ambition in life is, my ultimate ambition." He stopped there, perhaps for dramatic effect, perhaps

13

just to concentrate on removing the foil from his after-dinner cigar. "My ambition in life, and I'm telling you straight, is to live my life as much like Christ as possible."

I didn't doubt his sincerity. As he drove off later in his mauve Cadillac, I noticed a bumper sticker: "Smile, God Loves You." Well, it would be a pleasure to be rid of this kind of a luncheon, this kind of a man.

Back at the office there was a message. David Laventhol, the editor, had received my note of resignation and wanted to see me.

"You're not serious about this?" he said.

"Yes," I said. "I've really made up my mind this time."

"And there's nothing I can say that will change it?"

"No," I said.

"Very well, then I won't try."

In a way, I wish he *had* tried. There is nothing quite so deflating as a resignation that is too easily accepted. Laventhol and I had, twenty years earlier, gone to the same school together and put out the same college newspaper together. We were friends as well as associates, and it was not surprising that he said some nice things during this last meeting. Then he talked about a trend I was keenly aware of, the direction of newspapers in general toward the less fanciful; the aim was to be more responsive to specific news events.

The general-interest columnist had become less essential and I suspect the point of mentioning this was to let me know I might be doing the right thing. I realized that the general-interest columnist was the tap dancer of journalism, the frivolous entertainer who filled the spaces between more serious endeavors, but I thought none the less of him because of that.

We deal in whimsy and humor and all too often it seems that our fingers get stuck on the "I" key, which is why we have always been slightly suspect by our less whimsical cohorts. We have also become something of a vanishing breed.

In the era of Watergate, the spotlight had shifted onto the investigative reporter, the fact-gatherer able to come up with new evidence pointing up our most ancient failings. Well, that had never been for me. I had always responded more readily to a story offering a glimpse of the human soul than to a story recording one historic panorama or another. I took greater pleasure from a small

14

essay celebrating the first snowfall of winter than one summing up the arguments of any great debate. In choosing between reporter and writer, I would always take the writer—for the one, I feel respect; for the other, love.

"We're going to hate to see you go, though," Dave said. "Jesus, how long have you been with the paper anyway?"

It struck me then that I was sitting in the editor's office for the last time. I had been there scores of times in the past—asking to go after one story or another. I was never one of those columnists who felt that an event didn't happen unless I was there to cover it; nonetheless, I managed to wangle a front-row seat to most of the memorable events of the decade.

I had gone on that walk from Selma to Montgomery. I had watched us waging an incomprehensibly dirty war in Vietnam. I had witnessed the life cycles of both the civil-rights and the peace movements. Sitting there in the editor's office, I thought back to four days on the streets of Chicago during the 1968 political convention. I recalled writing about the assassination of our finest men and the elevation of those who represented what was worst in us.

I thought back a decade to a snowy night when my paper let me rent a suite at the Americana Hotel and invite seventy-five total strangers to a party; it was a hell of a party. I remembered playing Minnesota Fats in a friendly game of Eight Ball and beating him. The memories came fast and crowded out whatever Dave was saying, and suddenly tears started to roll down my cheeks.

I am not a weeper. In the past two decades I had only cried once before, at the death of a best friend, and now for no reason I could understand—it was, after all, *my* decision—I was crying. I became keenly aware of the plate-glass windows separating me from a city room filled with reporters. I wondered what they would think if they glanced our way, but I couldn't hold back the tears.

"This is the damndest thing," I said. "I mean, this is really something I want to do."

"Yeah," he said.

"I really am sorry about this," I said. "I'll get out of here in a minute. Just give me a minute and I'll get out."

"Take all the time you want," he said. "Take it easy."

15

I don't know who was more embarrassed by the tears. It all came down to the realization that I was turning my back on what had been the richest and most rewarding period in my life; I felt like a man abandoning a good and faithful woman for something he doesn't quite understand.

I finally exited by a rear door and walked through the city room to my own cubicle. Later in the day I was visited by publisher Bill Attwood, the former editor of *Look* magazine.

"I think it's wonderful news," he said.

"You do?"

"Sure," he said. "You're doing the right thing. I always try to change jobs every five years myself. It keeps you alive."

I wish everyone hadn't been so damn chipper about my departure. I felt like a man who had come to the painful decision to divorce his wife only to have everyone, including the wife, say, "Fine, wonderful, what else is new?"

That night I wanted to get home early and explain the situation to my three children. My plan was to reassure them that the loss of a job was not the end of the world, that Mommy was perfectly capable of being our breadwinner for a while. The important thing, I decided, was to keep it light and casual, to betray not the slightest hint of nervousness.

Before arriving home, however, I stopped at the neighborhood tavern, the Pier Three, where my friends had gathered to toast my decision. There were many toasts to a future that seemed uncertain at best. And it was a day of firsts for me. Just as I had never cried without apparent reason before, so I had never drunk myself insensible before. For the first time in my life, I blacked out.

Fortunately, Corinne was there to drive me home. I often wonder what she was thinking during that drive. She knew that my aim was to reassure the children—yet there I was beside her, snoring against the window pane. I wonder now whether she was aware of the fear I was feeling. We've never discussed the matter.

We arrived home and Corinne parked the car in the driveway. By this time I was unbudgeable. But it was November and cold and every hour or so she came out to make sure I hadn't frozen to death.

"Don't you want to come in?" she said during one body check.

"What I want most is to die."

16

"But didn't you want to talk to the kids?" she said. "Didn't you want to reassure them?"

"Reassure them?"

What the kids would have seen was a frightened, forty-year-old man facing a turning point in his life with an absolute minimum of grace, throwing up occasionally onto the driveway. All and all, it would not have been a terribly reassuring sight.

I had given the paper six weeks' notice and those final weeks are not numbered among my happiest ones at the paper. Before I started to clean out my desk, things began to disappear. One day I showed up for work and my typewriter had disappeared; taped to the typewriter table was a note from the editor who took it, saying I could borrow it back if I needed it for anything. The next day the table was gone.

No one waited for the corpse to grow cold. The struggle for the column began well before it was available. Within the paper itself there was naturally a spirited competition, and more than a few readers wrote letters similar to this one: "We know you'll miss Mike McGrady's column but maybe you'd like to fill it with a new kind of material, something more intellectual perhaps. I'm enclosing some samples . . ."

There was a splendid send-off, two hundred people filling the bar attached to a local bowling alley, nice words, a gift, kisses, and then it was over and I was on my own.

There were a couple of final mentions in the newspaper. The day after I left, my name appeared in a news story and it was a shock to see myself described as "former columnist Mike McGrady." That quickly. The words hits me with a strange impact. I could only be described as a former something because I was a current nothing, a suburban househusband.

And then a week after that there was a headline over the letters-to-the-editor page that said, "Farewell, Mike." Quite a few regular readers had gone to the trouble of writing in to say they were going to miss me. By that time, I was beginning to sense I would probably miss them more. There was one printed letter, I must say, that proved mildly infuriating. It was sent in by one of those thoroughly liberated women who didn't know my reasons for leaving the job and especially didn't know of my wish to free my wife completely of housewifely chores.

She wrote this: "Even though I have found some of Mike McGrady's entertaining columns slightly chauvinistic, I never tired of him."

Slightly chauvinistic—who, me?

THREE

Monday, January 14

We are to begin.

At seven o'clock this morning, an hour before my usual time of awakening, I hear a voice on the clock radio saying the temperature outside is twenty-four degrees, that the day will be clear and cold.

Today, it seems, marks the start of more than one great experiment. It is, to be sure, my debut as a male housewife. But it is also the beginning of a new national fuel-saving program; Congress has advanced Daylight Saving Time several months in order to extend our twilights. The immediate result, I learn, is that there is less light at the beginning of the day and the darkness this first morning is impressive. The porch lights must be turned on so that the three children can find their way to the bus stop over snow that has frozen into a white rockiness.

My announced intention was to send the kids off every day with a hot breakfast and a nutritious lunch. But this first morning we seem to be short on some supplies. As nearly as I can determine, there are no eggs, no bread, no butter, no milk. This makes breakfast something of a challenge and lunch an impossibility. What happens is that they are served cereal with powdered milk and given sufficient money to buy lunch in the school cafeteria.

There is still another impediment. Corinne's car has been starting sluggishly on cold mornings and we have made an appointment at the Volkswagen service center. The car is scheduled for an Early Bird Special, an eight o'clock service appointment.

One hitch here. It is a cold morning, precisely the kind of morning that causes the car to balk. As the children are stumbling toward the bus, grumbling to their friends about the taste of powdered milk, I am doing one of my least favorite tasks, hooking up battery cables from one car to another. The first car, my car, starts right up but, for one reason or another, seems reluctant to transmit any of its electrical power to its sister ship's battery. The cables are hooked up first this way, then that. Nothing. Next I bring out an electric blanket and a long extension cord.

My hands are numb and my nose is red and finally, shortly after nine, the car stops its whining, grumbles a few times, and kicks over. The sound awakens Corinne. It is the first morning in some time that she has not risen with the children and she seems relaxed.

"My hands are frozen," I say. "Those damn battery cables."

"Oh, I should have done that," she says. "That's the man's job."

"*Now* you tell me."

This is going to take some adjusting. I am wondering whether it will ever be possible to wake Corinne up with the words that most males have heard at one time or another: "My car won't start." I am wondering, furthermore, what *her* first words might be in response to an announcement of that nature. But surely even this is a matter of conditioning. It takes no great physical strength, no exclusively masculine talent, to hook up cables between batteries.

As Corinne's car continues to warm up, she pauses for a cup of coffee, packs up her business case, and we both start the drive to the Volkswagen place nearly ten miles away. While I go in to speak to the service manager, she remains in her car—I am secretly wondering whether she should be the one to go in and arrange the details, but I am not ready to suggest this.

"I'm sorry, Mr.—ah—McGrady," the service manager says, "but you have told us the car will be here at eight o'clock and, as you can see, it is now almost ten o'clock."

"Let me tell you the trouble again," I say. "The trouble with the car is that it doesn't start on a cold morning."

"Yes." He nods his head and smiles amiably. "Just so. That is what has been written in the service book."

"The car does not start on a cold morning," I proceed, "and this morning, you will remember, was a very cold morning, and the only reason we are late for this appointment is the very reason we have made this appointment."

19

"Just so," he says. "But today we are all booked up. I believe, however, we can fit you in as soon as Friday morning, early."

"And if Friday is a cold morning?"

"Well, then, we shall see."

"No." It strikes me that this conversation has gone far enough. "We shall see *now*. I made this appointment a week ago. At that time I told you what the trouble was and you're damn well going to take the car now."

Silence. It might be felt that a day that begins this badly can only improve, but, unfortunately, that has not always been my experience. In fact, life has taught me that any day that begins with battery cables is most often a day not worth getting up for. I am tempted at this juncture to stop, return to the car, suggest to Corinne that we wait one additional week before beginning our new life. However, I have delayed the start on two previous Mondays and after two false starts, I am determined to get on with it.

"We will compromise," the service manager finally decides. "We will say Friday but this time we will not make it Early Bird. How is that?"

"We will say today—how is that?"

"Very well, Mr. McGrady, we'll see what we can do."

I spend so much of my life not insisting on things that it is always a surprise to discover what a little insistence can accomplish. My sense of triumph lasts only until I reach the parked car, the impatient wife.

"That took forever," Corinne says.

"They didn't want to take your car," I explain. "They said we were too late."

"That's absurd," she says. "You should have told them it doesn't start on a cold morning."

"It'll be ready this afternoon after work," I say, ignoring that one.

"It's late," she says. "I've got to get a move on."

Corinne is feeling the press of time passing, and I'm impressed only by the vast space of time that lies directly ahead of me. Seconds, minutes, hours—an entire day of freedom. No obligations. No responsibilities. A Monday without a column to write. For once I do not have to get to the office early and check the wires and rush through the mail and come up with an idea that can be translated into seven hundred words before suppertime. There is an undeniable feeling of luxury—mingled with just a trace of compassion—as I drop Corinne off at her office.

"Don't forget Siobhan," she says.

"Siobhan what?"

"Her appointment with the orthodontist," she says. "You remember, she told you to pick her up at school at eleven o'clock."

"Oh." I had forgotten. "It's almost that now."

"Yes, you better run."

Okay, the orthodontist—how long could that take? Time to do the shopping and the cooking. Time left over for some things I haven't done in far too long. The library, a nice long game of pool, a few friendly belts at the Pier Three.

But first things first. The orthodontist. Since this is a man to whom I will be sending money every month for the next three years, it is not an appointment I am inclined to miss.

Although the day has heated all the way up to twenty-eight degrees, the Volkswagen heating plant is not all that it might be. I am keenly aware of the ten-minute wait for Siobhan outside her school and the twenty-minute drive to the dentist's office. He has not been waiting our arrival with baited breath—a half hour passes before he recognizes Siobhan's arrival and another half hour goes by before he escorts her into his office.

The waiting room seems to have been designed with women in mind. Something about the colors. And the magazines are all women's magazines. The other people in the waiting room are all women. I am self-conscious, as I've always been when I find myself temporarily lost in a female world, and I am wondering if this is something I will have to get used to.

I pick up the issue of *Vogue* and the feature article seems to be about golf: "Get Me to the Tee on Time." Actually, it's not about golf so much as it is about the kind of dresses women should wear to the course. Hey, that's something—this summer I'll find time for an occasional round of golf. The ads ("Give him something to reach for!") were not written with me in mind. In fact, the one section of the magazine that strikes home is my horoscope for the month of January—

"LIBRA: Give special consideration to ending one business and

21

entering another that is unusual, innovative, and something of a gamble. There may be two partners involved."

Does any time pass more slowly than the time spent in a dentist's waiting room? An hour stretches out endlessly. Yes, finally I have time. Time to exhaust the magazines on the rack, time to study the frayed spots in the once golden wall-to-wall carpeting, time to count the lipstick-smeared cigarette butts in the ashtrays, time to study the broken slats in the venetian blinds.

The piped-in music, a million tinkling pianos, may have been selected for its pain-killing qualities but surely not for any time-killing property. I am starting to go quietly crazy staring at mountain-studded, lake-pocked landscape prints that are useful only to the extent they take your mind off the wallpaper. Well, this will be the last time for this particular experience. This will be the last time I wait while anyone has braces tightened. Braces tightened? He is taking all this time to adjust a few pieces of wire? Surely there has been sufficient time to remove a brain tumor.

Then, finally, I turn off. The wait becomes long, then unendurable, then impossible, and finally I give up; I lose hope in hope. And I have seen the first hours of my new life slip through my fingers as irretrievably as grains of sand. At that moment the door to the cubicle opens and Siobhan emerges, flashing a silvery smile of relief. I am reminded: it has been worse for her.

"Siobhan has been a naughty girl," the orthodontist says. "She has been eating the wrong things."

"I'll talk to her about that."

"She really shouldn't eat apples."

"No apples. Okay."

"And that goes for potato chips, too."

"No potato chips."

"She's got a list," he says. "You should ask Mrs. McGrady to check on it."

He rattles on and on. Can't he see how anxious I am to get out of his office, to escape this particular level of hell? No, wait, before leaving we must make an appointment for the next visit. In two weeks. *Two* weeks? That soon?

"How's a Wednesday afternoon for Mrs. McGrady?" the receptionist is asking me.

"Pardon me."

22

"How's Wednesday for Mrs. McGrady?" she says. "For the next appointment, will a Wednesday be all right for Mrs. McGrady?"

"I'm the one who'll be bringing Siobhan in," I say, "and Wednesday should be all right."

As I drive Siobhan back to school, I am again aware of time escaping. My intention was to make the first dinner something truly memorable. But now my feeling is that I don't want to take any unnecessary risks; I will try something I've done before. A rib roast. Never mind that this will bust my budget the very first night, the important thing is that dinner get made and the other important thing is that it not be too unimpressive.

As I go to the supermarket, I sense a small problem with the money. The problem is this: Corinne has forgotten to give it to me. Well, okay. I have not yet forgotten how to write a check against my own account.

The first thing I notice in the supermarket is that something has happened to the prices. I have always been something of a cottage-cheese freak and the last time I purchased cottage cheese it was thirty-four cents for the pound container, fifty-nine cents for the two-pound container. Well, I pick up the pound container and it says fifty-nine cents and I think someone has made a mistake in pricing. But I check the other containers—the two-pound size is marked "$1.29"—and I realize it is not a misprint. I purchase neither.

The roast beef has undergone a similar elevation and now comes to eleven dollars for a piece of meat that will barely withstand a five-way division. I throw in some potatoes, carrots, onions, bread and milk and a twenty-dollar bill does not cover the tab.

How long has this been going on? I am feeling a kinship to Rip Van Winkle as I settle back into the car and remember that I have gotten nothing for dessert. I had originally planned on a chocolate mousse, but there will be no time for that. What I do, instead, is stop at the bakery and spring for eclairs stuffed with whipped cream. Forty cents each. Forty cents *each!* I can't get over what has happened to food prices.

The food is rushed home, put in the refrigerator. By this time—and it is past two—I am scrambling, trying to salvage a few

23

hours from a day that is shrinking at an alarming rate. The house seems unnaturally dark and quiet, almost spooky. I realize then how few times I've seen it deserted. In an hour the kids will be home from school and the lights will be burning and the mayhem will begin; but now it seems just slightly pathetic.

I had planned to pass at least a half day in the library, a leisurely hour or two at the magazine rack before moving on to a tour of the stacks. The moment I walk into the library, I do feel, for the first time, a sense of some of the rewards awaiting me in this new life. I am one of those people whose love of books extends beyond the reading of them—I like to pick them up and hold them and weigh them in my hands. The library is a treasure house filled with the books there has been no time to read in the scramble of my recent years. The only difficulty is in finding a starting point. Everywhere I look there is a title I've been promising myself to read.

When I see the Kosinski novel, *Steps,* I reach out for it. I'd wanted to read the book some years earlier—God, *five* years earlier—when it won the National Book Award. Better late than never. My library card is found buried beneath the credit cards and handed over to the librarian.

"Your card is out of date," she says.

"Oh?"

"Three years out of date," she says.

She gives me the special look she reserves for Philistines, then types out my new library card, the one that will surely wear out from the use I intend to give it. Ten minutes later, the book under my arm, I stop for still another brand-new luxury, a friendly little belt with the boys at Pier Three.

Well, the Pier is not the same place in the afternoon. Possibly because the boys are all out working. There is Linda, the barmaid, and myself, and a young man who is a patient at the nearby veterans hospital. He has somehow come up with the notion that everyone is able to listen to his thoughts and, beyond that, has gone to the trouble of tuning in on his mind.

"You know what I'm thinking, don't you?" he says to me.

"No."

"Yes you do," he says.

"Okay."

24

"I don't mind your knowing what I'm thinking," he says. "Just don't tell Linda."

"What?"

"Don't tell Linda what I'm thinking."

"Okay."

Now he is right; I do know what he is thinking. He is thinking just what 95 per cent of the patrons at the Pier Three are thinking at any given moment. Which is just what they would like to do to Linda under the proper circumstances. When Linda's sister, Betty, is on duty, they are thinking what they would like to do to Betty.

"What time is it?" I ask Linda.

"Four-thirty," she says.

"Fine, you can pour me another," I say. "Hey, Linda, how long does it take to cook a roast beef."

"What kind of a roast?"

"A rib roast."

"Oh, yeah, that's about twenty minutes a pound, for medium."

Twenty minutes a pound. For medium. Okay, then, it is an eight-pound rib roast. Let me see. That means it will take 160 minutes. That breaks down to . . . oh . . . two hours and forty minutes. *Two hours and forty minutes!* One of my resolutions was to have dinner ready at six o'clock every night. If I leave the Pier at this moment, I will be home at five, and dinner should be ready at . . . oh . . . eight o'clock. I go for the phone.

"Hello," Siobhan says.

"Hello, darling," I say. "How would you like to do Daddy a little favor?"

"It depends," she says.

"It depends on what, darling?"

"It depends on what you mean by little."

"Oh, it's nothing," I say. "Just go to the refrigerator and take the big roast beef and put it in the oven and put the heat up to 350 degrees."

"That's a *big* favor," she says. "I'm not even sure I can remember all that."

I am talking to an "A" student who has just celebrated her thirteenth birthday. She has one of the most well-organized minds it has ever been my pleasure to observe, and one day she will be a first-rate lawyer; I am trying to imagine the difficulty she will have performing this simple task.

"I'll pay you a quarter," I say.

"One quarter?"

"No, sweetheart," I say. *"Two* quarters. But for two quarters you also have to have the potatoes and carrots and onions peeled by the time I get home."

"I hate to peel onions," she says. "They make me cry."

"Okay," I say. "Just the potatoes and carrots then, but please have them done by the . . ."

The deal has been made. Still, I hurry the drink and make my way home as rapidly as possible. By the time I've traveled the ten miles home, I'm feeling better. Even better when I pick up the hearty smell of beef roasting. But not too much better because my daughter greets me with a message: "Mommy says don't forget to pick her up after work."

It's back to the car, back to town and Corinne's office, back again on the road. Finally, putting the car away for the night, I notice that the total mileage for the day is more than one hundred, more than it would have been had I taken the thirty-mile drive to the newspaper office and back.

I'm finally relaxed. The potatoes and carrots have been peeled and are ready to be popped in the oven beside the beef. I slip Siobhan two quarters.

"Well, you seem to have everything under control," Corinne says.

"Nothing to it."

"How did your day go?

"Just fine," I say. "I did some shopping—I can't get over how much prices have risen."

"Is that a hint?" she says. "Well, I've already made out your check—it's in my purse."

"Oh, I don't know that we have to start right out . . ."

"A deal's a deal," she says.

The check is for a hundred dollars. It is an unpracticed exchange, accomplished awkwardly. I don't know which of us has more difficulty, which of us is more embarrassed. I guess Corinne handles her side of the exchange more smoothly than I do. Corinne was raised in a well-to-do family and, during the normal

26

rebellions of adolescence, she rebelled against money—decided then that money would never become of paramount importance to her. I must say that she has stuck to that.

It is the easiest hundred dollars I've ever made. But the reversal feels strange. In a marriage of any duration, the two people become tied together by hundreds of threads—habits, understandings, obligations—and a single strand would not seem to matter all that much. But the money thread does. This ritual, the giving of allowance by one human being to another, bespeaks whole planets of meaning; it has to do with independence, gratification, reward, punishment, resentment. The feelings are so intertwined that I doubt whether they can be fully understood until the situation is reversed. Believe me, when the child starts to give the parent an allowance, whole worlds shatter.

My own reaction on receiving money—this first day and every week since then—has not been what I anticipated. It is not a pleasurable experience, not in the least. In fact, there is on my part inevitably an effort to minimize the transaction, to snatch up the check and stuff it into my wallet as rapidly as possible, to pretend that the transaction doesn't really matter. I can see, in Corinne, opposite tendencies, an effort to ceremonialize the offering, to announce it in advance—"Ah, today is the day you get your allowance"—to make a production number out of locating the checkbook and the pen, to sign it with a flourish, to hand it over with a kiss.

I know her feeling all too well. I'm sure there is at least a small sensation of triumph in turning the tables after all these years. And surely there is a strong element of pride—after all, she is pulling not only her weight but *our* weight. And maybe, just maybe, there is a trace element of resentment—as in, "Why should I have to take care of everyone else?" I know how hard it can be to make a hundred dollars, how much work it can represent, but if Corinne has ever felt those feelings, she has not allowed them to surface.

"Are you sure this is going to be enough?" she says.

"It looks like a lot to me."

"Wait until Friday." The voice of experience. "It won't look like so much then."

"I feel funny taking it," I admit. "And I hate to think of you having to pay the bills."

"I wanted to speak to you about that," she says.

She sits down with me then at the dining room table and takes out a small stack of envelopes with windows. I still hate the sight of them. I am wondering how she is reacting to paying the telephone bill ($54.71) and the gas bill ($48.45) and the electric bill ($82.34).

"This lighting bill," she says.

"Yes."

"It's for November-December," she says. "It's your bill."

"Well, it just arrived on Saturday," I explain. "That makes it a January bill."

"No," she says. "It says right here—'November-December'— and that makes it your bill. And the Exxon bill is for oil that was delivered in December. And this Bloomingdale's bill has gone on for three months."

"Well, if it's going to be too difficult for you to pay the bills . . ."

"No one is saying that anything is going to be too difficult," she says. "It's just that we said I'd pay all the bills *after* January first and, as you can see, these were all run up before January first."

The business transactions between man and wife add up to the least pleasant part of any marriage. What happens—and doubtless what should happen—is that I wind up retrieving my checkbook from semi-retirement and writing out checks that come to $356 and change. Just as in the good old days.

Dinner is late but satisfactory. There is nothing to criticize about the roast beef—it is deep brown on the outside, pink on the inside, tender and succulent. The potatoes seem a trifle on the hard side but, as I demonstrate for three skeptical children, they can be rendered edible by simply mashing them down into the beef drippings. There is no salad, no green vegetables, but the eclairs offer some compensation.

So, during this first day, I have cooked the first of many dinners; I have received my first allowance check; I have suffered a net financial loss of $256; I have driven 108 miles, and I haven't had more than a few minutes to myself. But a car has gotten to a service center, a daughter has gotten to the dentist and a dinner has

28

gotten to the table. And at the end of the day I have a book to read, one that I've been looking forward to for five years.

Yes. And by ten o'clock the dishes are done and everyone is in bed and I open up the book. I manage to read two paragraphs before my eyes become heavy and I feel myself slipping off to sleep.

One down—how many to go?

FOUR

Cooking would be a snap. I sensed that some aspects of my new life—cleaning, laundering, child-rearing—might present an occasional challenge, but cooking held no terror for me.

In my bachelor years, I had even fancied myself something of a chef. By my twentieth year I had developed and perfected a spaghetti sauce that has not had to be altered significantly since, and it was then, at that tender age, that I learned to whip up a tunafish salad that will still lend luster to any sandwich.

This early interest in cuisine was by no means accidental. By then I had discovered that the shortest distance to almost anyone's heart was via the stomach; when the man was doing the cooking, there was an added ingredient: novelty. I found few sights more memorable than the way a young woman's eyes would soften in the flickering light cast by a duck flambé.

My repertoire, though impressive enough in its particulars, now seems laughably limited in range. It is quite possible that the reason Corinne and I are married today is because I proposed so rapidly, before having run through the eight dishes I had mastered.

During the six months following marriage, the list expanded. Out of necessity. There I was, living with a twenty-year-old girl who had, until then, been attending college, majoring in existential philosophy and Far Eastern religions. Clearly, the cooking would be up to me. And during our first six months together, I, in fact, did do all the cooking. Money was a problem and much of my early culinary pioneering was in the frankfurter field.

29

In those days, a time of great nutritional innocence, our diet would be supplemented once or twice a week with frozen fare, quite often frozen chicken pies. Catsup was not so much a condiment as a necessity, a cover-up for a countless string of miscalculations. But somehow—relying on friends, on luck, on the Swanson frozen-food people, on a few cheap cuts of meat—we got by.

Then Corinne made her fatal error. One night, midway through our first year of marriage, I was working late and hard—typing up a short story that the *Saturday Evening Post* had agreed to buy if I would only add "a secondary love interest." That night Corinne volunteered to cook a meal, to put together a little something out of lamb shanks, yams, green beans, and lemon juice.

A triumph. The dish was imaginative, delicious, easy on the eyes and the stomach, and cheap. How good was it? I can perhaps best describe the quality of that meal by pointing out, simply, that it would be fifteen years before another meal would be prepared under my personal direction.

What happened was not at all unusual, was the very opposite of unusual. We simply slipped into the roles that had been scripted for us during the past many generations. Male and Female. I made the living—first by writing children's books and short stories for slick magazines and then one day, with the third child due to arrive, I went out and sought a salaried job with the nearest newspaper.

Corinne played Female. That is to say, she stayed home with the children and did the cleaning and the cooking. It is, in retrospect, incredible that she did all this routinely and without complaint. She was twenty years old, an artist good enough to have had several formal shows, a student in the middle of her education, and one day she agreed to take on a lifelong job that few servants would tackle. She did it because it was expected, because it was what every other woman did.

And since she was an artist, since she was gifted and creative, she not unnaturally attempted to apply her skills to her new life as housewife. It was a little like asking a nuclear physicist to apply his talents to sweeping public streets. She did well at the most mundane tasks, very well indeed, but who can measure the toll? Not just the toll in years—for these could have been her most productive years—but a toll in spirit. There were rough times, times when in the middle of the night she would flee family and house, get in the car and drive for hours along shore roads. There were other times when her patience would be worn thin as gauze and that normally well-modulated voice turned into something out of a low-budget horror movie.

Still and all, as a housewife she was a resounding success. For the better part of a decade she did all that the world expected and more. On many aspects of housewifery there is no sure way to judge success or failure, but with cooking the reaction is instantaneous and hard to disguise.

It is, too, the part of keeping a home, the *one* part, that demands creativity. When you dust a table, there is no reason to do it a different way every time; but each meal sets up a different set of problems and solutions. This is quite likely why Corinne was such a superb cook from the beginning and why, as time passed, she devoted more and more of her energy to cooking—going so far as to make her own pasta, to grow her own herbs and spices, to find shops that carried such things as organically grown vegetables or exotic oriental specialties.

With the pressures of the new life, pressures prompted by society's expectations, Corinne soon abandoned such extraneous endeavors as painting, sculpting, studying and working. The one place she could deposit her artistic impulses was the dinner table—and what dinners she made! Among our friends, she quickly earned a reputation as a splendid cook and it was not long before that reputation grew and near strangers would angle for dinner invitations.

There was no longer any need for me to waste my increasingly valuable time cooking, and there was something intimidating about competing with someone that accomplished. The solution was obvious; I stopped cooking. And cleaning. And changing diapers. And staying around the house where these things were most likely to be done.

Not that Corinne was ever content to be a housewife. She found spare hours for child-oriented projects, for a co-operative nursery school, for starting a Montessori school that still flourishes today. Under her watchful eyes, the children were growing up well and well loved, and my presence was something of a redundancy.

And if, through all those years, she was going quietly batty, who would ever know about it? Outsiders didn't see the temper flare-ups, the moments of deep despondency. They didn't see this and I didn't quite understand it; at such times I would pitch in a little and try to shoulder some of the burdens. I discovered that what kept her happy, or at least occupied, was the prospect of designing a new bedroom or adding a new kitchen or figuring out the plan for a whole new wing. As the years went by, the house grew and grew.

Perhaps I never even saw the worst moments. After all, there was a ladder to climb, income levels to reach, and a job that was cancer to my spare time. And all the while I could congratulate myself on my good fortune, on having a mate who was also a manager, a woman who could run a house and a husband and a family, enabling all of us to reach our potentials. Well, *almost* all of us.

At times I felt pangs of guilt. Other men might buy their wives a diamond ring or a fur coat or take a sudden trip to Puerto Rico. When the guilt got the better of me, I would suggest to Corinne that it was time to put on the new bedroom, the new patio, and new shed, and somehow we would make it into the next year. If the guilt became too strong, I would remind myself that Corinne was five years younger and that she would have plenty of time, at some indefinite future date, to realize her potential, whatever that might be. Yes, there would be plenty of time for her when the children were grown and out.

It was Corinne who finally upset this image by forcibly changing the patterns herself. I recall a turning point came when she read *The Feminine Mystique*. It was not that the complaints were novel or that someone had finally articulated the problem. No, it was the discovery that she had company, plenty of company, out there, and that, furthermore, she was part of a system that was being kept alive without the consent of the governed.

Before a problem can be solved, it must be identified. The solutions—those solutions that might work for us—became apparent a half-dozen years ago when I took a year's sabbatical to go to Harvard. Corinne registered at the Harvard School of Design and began to mix with young people who shared her interests. Hardly by coincidence, she at this point expanded her business from plastic jewelry to home furnishings. Quite consciously she turned toward the outside world and, in so doing, turned her back on the house.

Suddenly the house was no longer spotless; the children were left to their own designs; the dinner table became something of a deprived area.

During the subsequent years of adjustment, it was clearly my responsibility to take up some of the slack. I tried—but it didn't work. I had lost all interest in cooking and somewhere through the passage of time, my old recipes had lost their magic; any dish calling for catsup or A.1. sauce as a main ingredient seemed less than impressive. But after a day at an office and an hour on a crowded highway, anything fancier seemed out of the question.

Well, that was all behind us now. With the new system I would have time to do something more than just shove food onto a plate. Each meal would be an event. Not just dinner—but breakfast and lunch as well.

The first meal—roast beef—had been satisfactory but not terribly impressive. It is difficult to go too far astray with a rib roast and even the children sensed that there was nothing overly complicated about putting a piece of meat in the oven and taking it out some time later. On the second night I was resolved to knock their eyes out.

Oysters Rockefeller, no less. My first shock that second day was the discovery that oysters now cost $4.25 a quart. Well, cost be hanged! This meal would be something special and there was something about this combination of ingredients—oysters, crumbled bacon, chopped greens, seasoned bread crumbs, a dash of anise—that seemed foolproof. All I would need were the ingredients and a blender.

When the blender blade broke, undoubtedly a victim of the same ailment that felled the waterbed, the dishwasher and the electric typewriter a day earlier, there was a bad moment or two. But I rationalized it in this manner: it was quite likely that man invented oysters Rockefeller before inventing the blender, and a little manual labor, a little chopping by hand, would probably improve the texture of the dish.

The children, unaccustomed to the sight of a man in Mommy's

33

kitchen, gathered around the chopping block and studied my every move. Their reaction was not exactly uncritical.

"Oh no," said Liam, eleven. "Not oysters."

"I don't want to hear that," he was told.

"They're gloopy," Siobhan said.

"Enough!"

"Well, they *are!*"

It is always easier to let the wind out of the sails than to gather it up. Since that evening, the phenomenon has repeated itself many times, more times than I care to admit or think about, and still it is not the kind of criticism that rolls off my back. The reason it always cuts deep is that cooking is the one area where a housewife is graded most severely.

"The worst part," Siobhan was saying, "is when you try to swallow them. It's like swallowing . . ."

"Siobhan . . ." I warned her.

". . . snot!" Liam finished her sentence.

"Okay, that's it." I stopped the chopping. "That's enough. We are going to get this straight right now. We are *not* going to be eating the same kind of food we've been eating the past few years. So long as I've got to cook meals every night, I'm going to try and do something special. This is the beginning of a new experiment and I do not intend to waste my time making the same old stuff every night—in fact, I'd like to go through the whole year and not serve the same dinner twice."

"Do you mean steak too?" Liam asked.

"What?"

"You mean we're only going to have steak once all year?"

"That's okay," his sister said. "That means we're only going to have oysters once and they're gloopy."

"There's no such word as gloopy," I said. "At least not around here, not any more. As long as I'm going to all this trouble, I would appreciate it if you'd go to the trouble of not saying gloopy, at least not until you've tried them."

"But what if I already know?" Siobhan said. "What if I already know that oysters make me throw up?"

"That's just fine," I said. "Just don't let me catch anyone throwing up *before* they've tried the dinner."

When the three of them realized that oysters were going to be served, no matter what, they deserted me. Ah, nothing to it. The ingredients were fried, dried, boiled, chopped, and carefully arranged, ready to go into the oven at an instant's notice. The rice was done to perfection and the butter was melting into it and, after popping the oysters into the oven, I broke open a nicely chilled bottle of chablis; no harm in an early sample. As the oysters began to broil, the kitchen was filled with the aroma of exotic spices. The chablis was light on the palate. This one, I told myself, would be a success. Was there anything wrong, anything missing? Yes. Corinne.

But it was seven-thirty, a full hour beyond the scheduled dinnertime. Where could she be? I quickly turned off an oven containing a platter of oysters Rockefeller cooked to perfection and dialed Corinne's office.

"Oh," she said. "I got so busy I didn't see the time. I'll leave in a few minutes.

"The dinner is done," I said.

"I'm on my way."

A half-hour later, hearing the sound of a car coming up the driveway, I once again turned on the oven. The passage of time had done very little for the oysters. What it had done for them, to be precise, is to shrivel them up.

I served them in silence. There is not much to be said about oysters that are shriveled and I didn't trust myself to speak right then. Corinne, too, was silent, possibly because she realized that the condition of the oysters could be linked to her time of arrival. One thing I will say, however, I have never seen oysters anywhere that anyone was less apt to describe as gloopy.

"Ummm," Corinne finally found words. "I just love oysters Rockefeller."

Was that sufficient? Not quite. Possibly only an ultra-sensitive cook would realize that phrase is not necessarily a compliment. On this particular night, I was listening to every word.

"I know you love oysters Rockefeller," I said, "but how do you like *these* oysters Rockefeller?"

"They're very interesting." Corinne has trouble fibbing and she seemed to be in some difficulty. "What did you do to them?"

"What I did to them was cook them a goddamned hour too long."

35

I stopped then and none too soon. The three children, lacking either Corinne's guilt or her generosity of spirit, were staring at their plates as though I had just slipped them three portions of green poison.

"Taste it," I commanded. "If you don't at least taste it, how're you going to know if you like it or not."

"I'll taste it," Siobhan said, "and then I'm going to throw up."

"If you throw up, little princess, then you're not going to get dessert."

"There's dessert too?"

Did I detect a note of fear in Corinne's voice? Yes, indeed there was a dessert to look forward to, a nice chocolate mousse. And here I have had the foresight to rely on Craig Claiborne, the food expert from the New York *Times* and the author of a cookbook I have used almost every day for one dish or another. Claiborne is my new hero, my main man, and his book had not one, but two recipes for chocolate mousse. There was "Mousse I" and "Mousse II." "Mousse I" is the easy version, the one that is whipped up in a blender; "Mousse II" calls for some complicated cooking, involving double boilers and requiring twelve hours to settle properly once it is done.

An hour before dinner, upon learning that the blender was not going to be working, I tried to do what every good cook does—improvise. I decided to combine the two recipes. Since the blender was malfunctioning, I'd melt the chocolate (as in "Mousse II") and then simply stir things up by hand. I soon learned that there was no easy way to fold the egg whites into the dense chocolate mixture by hand and I couldn't have been more surprised when the resulting blend turned out to be gray instead of the traditional brown.

Now I divided this slightly unorthodox treat into five equal portions and set it out in front of each member of the family and waited for them to dig in. And waited. And waited. As it turned out, I became the only man in history to ever make a dessert out of chocolate that my children refused to eat.

"*This* is gloopy," Siobhan said.

It was a rocky beginning, but it was a beginning. Since then no one has actually thrown up as a direct result of my cooking, and I will say, in all modesty, that if there has been any aspect of my new life that is a success, it is the cooking. I have taken to reading cookbooks with the kind of avidity I formerly reserved for a John Cheever novel. I've learned that there is no reason to have a simple pork chop when with just a little more effort you can have an herbed pork chop.

The cookbook collection now numbers in the dozens, but the one I've come back to time and time again is good old Craig Claiborne. He is reliable. Other cookbooks tend to promise more than you can deliver or else they go on for pages, one complicated set of instructions after another. With Craig it is hard to go wrong. Well, let me say this—feel free to skip past his curry recipes. But almost everything else is both simple and at least slightly elegant.

One of Craig's truly solid recipes is his cheese soufflé. I have made it a half-dozen times without a miss; each time the soufflé has been an airy triumph, toasted on the outside, creamy on the inside. Cooking, however, is fun only when it is experimental; it goes against the grain to repeat the same recipe every time out. And on this particular night I decided to try another soufflé, what Julia Child refers to as her "noncollapsible soufflé."

"Noncollapsible soufflé"—the name itself inspires confidence. And reading about what is going to happen will put the least experienced cook's mind at ease. For one thing, the soufflé does not have to be served immediately—according to the book, it can be cooked and then kept warm for half an hour without relinquishing any of its charm. Moreover, the soufflé is guaranteed not to stick to the sides of the dish and can, in fact, be turned upside down onto a serving platter without losing its shape.

What causes all these miracles? Well, the major difference between the "noncollapsible" and other soufflés is that this one is baked in a double pan, the outer pan filled with water. The water apparently slows down the cooking process, because the "noncollapsible" cooks for a full hour and a quarter at 350 degrees before you take it out and place it before your delighted family.

I will confess now to some skepticism. I was still a novice and it seemed to me that any egg mixture that cooked all that time surrounded by water would surely come out slightly soggy. But these dark thoughts dissipated whenever I conjured up Julia Child's broad, smiling, friendly, reassuring face as it appeared so frequently on television.

I told Corinne about the "noncollapsible soufflé" and she, too, had trouble understanding the underlying scientific principles. But I went ahead anyway and after an hour of baking the soufflé, I turned on the oven light and peeked in through the viewing window. I was somewhat surprised to see that nothing was rising above the rim of the pan and I was tempted, briefly, to open the door and examine the dish more closely. No, I knew better than to open an oven door just as a soufflé is mustering up its energy to rise and I did nothing to disturb the ascension.

As the hour and a quarter came to an end, I summoned the family and got the serving platter. True, the book said I could wait still another half-hour before serving the soufflé but I didn't want to press my luck. I wanted to serve it at the perfect moment, the moment of its apex, that fleeting instant when the wave is at its crest.

Not only had the soufflé not risen, it seemed to have sunk deeper into the pan, as if cowering in its own shame. When I turned it over, it flopped out and quivered, a leaden, soggy pancake of eggs, cheese, and mushrooms, your basic complete culinary disaster. It was clear that the "noncollapsible soufflé" was the greatest misnomer since someone named a ship *Titanic*.

What would Julia Child have done at such a moment? I could imagine her on television, making a funny face and coming up with a quick one-liner, then calmly dumping the entire mess into the nearest garbage can before trotting off to the next project. What did Mike McGrady do at such a moment? Ignoring the pained expressions surrounding him, he divided the mess into five equal parts and served it for dinner. And for once he did not try to stop his daughter as she, without a word, got up and started to make a tuna-fish sandwich.

Well, that, too, is part of cooking, and I have come to be philosophical about the disasters, to accept the fact that in every cook's life an occasional soufflé must fall. Learning how to cook has been a slow but sometimes rewarding process. It has been, in a sense, like modeling in clay. I have never in my life made something of clay that in any way resembled the original model but that hasn't stopped me from playing with clay and enjoying it.

Cooking can be creative, can tax the imagination, can lead to applause, and is the one aspect of being a housewife that has gotten more interesting as the year has progressed. The disasters have been outnumbered by the triumphs, and I can recall, with little urging, many good meals and some fine ones.

The four-day July Fourth weekend represented a kind of midyear test for a starting cook. On three of the four nights we had more than thirty guests, and on the final night, with the largest crowd of the weekend on hand, I settled for a huge pot of chili and a huge bowl of cole slaw. Not a particularly difficult dinner to cook but one that allows for a few nice touches. Instead of grinding the meat, for example, I chopped it by hand, and with cole slaw there are many possibilities.

Anyway, this time it was an unqualified crowd pleaser, and when I saw career dieters going back for third helpings I felt that warm glow that any performer feels when he is summoned for a curtain call. As dinner ended, as everyone sat there cleaning the final scraps from each bowl, I finally had a chance to sit down and rest.

Corinne chose this moment to come out of retirement. Incidentally, until then she had been the object of many admiring—one might even say envious—glances over the holiday weekend. There she was, moving her chaise longue to a shady spot while her husband slaved away to feed the multitudes. But now I looked up to see Corinne making the coffee.

It was the kind of gesture I might have made in years gone by, and when I saw her emerge from the kitchen carrying the ancient thirty-cup coffee maker, I decided to give her precisely the kind of treatment she might have given me.

"Will you look at that!" I said. "Will you look at what Corinne has done!"

"Oh, stop, Michael . . ."

"You did that all by yourself?" I said. "You took that water and that coffee and you did that without any help? With those two little hands, you went and . . . and these people thought Corinne didn't know how to cook." Oh, there was no stopping me. "Look what she has managed to do without any of my help. And just when we figured she was all through, all washed up, that she had lost her touch."

The guests gathered around to join in the merriment, to sample the coffee that those two delicate little hands had made, and with proper ado, without ever stopping my line of lavish praise, I turned the small spigot on the bottom of the urn and what came out was a stream of clear, colorless liquid. Hot water.

"I must have done something wrong," Corinne said.

"She has been away from this for some time," I apologized to the guests. "You'll have to forgive her—but I'll try to set it straight."

"I can't imagine what happened," Corinne said.

"Nice try, honey."

To this date I don't know what went wrong with the ancient coffee maker—maybe it was just a bit of temperament—but it worked perfectly when I tried the second batch. I'm sure that everyone has by now forgotten the incident, everyone with the possible exception of the cook and his helper. To me, it was one of the nice moments.

I'm not the first husband to take on the cooking, or at least a share of it. Most men who have tried to participate in a modern marriage know enough to assume at least a percentage of the responsibility.

My good friend Pat Owens, a fellow pool player and columnist, is one who has adjusted to the changing times by becoming something of a chef. And our conversations, the conversations of two fairly liberated husbands, often get into a discussion of culinary matters.

On this particular afternoon, Pat and I had just completed our weekly game of hundred-ball call shot, and after the game we adjourned next door to the Pier Three. As we walked in, Linda, the barmaid, reached for the scotch and the Bourbon.

"Better make it a double," Pat said.

"Times two."

Well, that's the way it always starts at the Pier Three. The conversation there was at its standard high level. There was some debate about whether it was appropriate to serve pizza on St. Patrick's Day. Then, too, there was the traditional speculation as to whether the old New York Yankees were better than the old Brooklyn Dodgers. And someone finally told us the true reason they closed down the exotic-dancers joint up the road.

At six o'clock Linda went off and Betty came on. The drinks had started to take hold and after a few double slams we slowed down to singles, with the house purchasing more than its share, as usual. Pat started looking to his watch.

"I've got to get home early this evening," he said. "It's my turn to cook and I've got to cook up some chicken for the boys."

"Yeah, what kind of chicken?"

"Roasting chicken," he said. "Hey, how do you roast a chicken anyway?"

"I tried it a new way last weekend," I told him. "I used this recipe from Craig Claiborne and it was the old Pennsylvania Dutch way. What they do is put mashed potatoes in the stuffing. Sensational."

"Well, I don't have time for that," Pat said. "I guess I'll do my chicken rosemary again."

"Chicken rosemary?"

"It's really very simple," he said. "You broil the chicken with rosemary all over it. I think I've found the big secret about cooking chicken anyway. Lots of butter, lots of lemon, lots of salt and pepper."

It was time for another round of drinks. The trick is to keep that edge without slipping off the bar stool. Though I hasten to add right here that slipping off a bar stool has never been regarded as a major *faux pas* in the Pier Three. In fact, it is the person who spends a great deal of time there without ever slipping off a bar stool who is most apt to raise suspicions.

"I've got to cook this Saturday," Pat was saying. "We've got some people coming over—hey, how do you make that steak Diane again?"

Ever since I had taken over the cooking at home, people had been asking me about my recipe for steak Diane.

"The thing is," I said, "you make sure the steak is sliced very thin. Then you hit it with a mallet until it's like paper. In a saucepan you start with a quarter pound of butter, put in some chopped shallots and parsley, add a dash of Tabasco sauce and a good blast of A.1. sauce . . ."

"A.1. sauce?" Pat said, just the slightest edge of criticism in his voice.

"Yeah, don't let anyone see you do that," I said. "Then you do

41

the steaks real quick at a high temperature, swish some sherry around the frying pan and add that to the sauce. Then if you want to serve it flambé—flaming, you know—you get some cognac and . . ."

I stopped right there. It had gotten very quiet in the old Pier Three. There was a long row of unshaven faces staring at us and I began to think what the whole conversation must have sounded like. I mean, it was just the normal after-hours conversation of two liberated husbands, but how do you explain that? Women's liberation is a good and necessary thing, long overdue, but there are some problems connected with it that have not been straightened out.

FIVE

During the first month of the year, Liam, our youngest, celebrated his eleventh birthday. This year, for the first time, I was in charge of buying all gifts. Although this was a situation that would lead, late in November, to my giving serious consideration to canceling Christmas, it was not too bad at the beginning of the year.

In fact, at my first stop I found the perfect gift. A model airplane with a gas engine, a beautifully detailed biplane with preassembled motor, bottled fuel, and complete instructions. The plane was an instantaneous hit.

"Can we put it together today?" Liam asked. "I want to see it fly."

The dinner table was quickly cleared of cake dishes, and together we spread out the plans. I began to wonder whether the fact that the model was a biplane might represent a tactical error on my part. There were dozens of sections that had to be put together, some with glue, others with thread. Bravely we went ahead, threading tiny holes, hooking braces together, tying dozens of knots.

"It won't take too long now," I said.

I said that several times during the course of the evening, and

42

then it hit me: What in the hell was I doing? This was clearly a man's job. Corinne was, at the time, sitting in an easy chair, enjoying a small luxury we don't usually have, an end-day cup of coffee. She seemed deeply involved with the evening newspaper.

"Oh, honey . . ."

"Yes?"

"When you get a minute, would you like to help Liam put together his new airplane. I'm all thumbs."

"I don't have the slightest idea how to do that."

"Putting together a model airplane is a father's job," I said. "This airplane is just too complicated for a little old housewife like myself."

"Not now, Michael." Whenever Corinne calls me Michael, her patience is wearing thin. "I'm really too tired to play games tonight."

"I'm sure Liam won't mind waiting until tomorrow," I said. "Tomorrow morning before you go to work."

"Tomorrow happens to be a very busy day."

I looked to Liam, then to the mess in front of us. There would be another hour, maybe two, of gluing together parts and hooking up threads and trying to figure out the fuel container. And then what? Then I could see us going down to the beach parking lot in the morning and launching the tiny biplane and then I could see us watching it tailspin to the pavement and crashing into splinters, just as all the other model planes did. This, this was a pleasure that surely belonged to Corinne.

"You'll have to speak to your mother," I told Liam.

"Michael, I'm really not in the mood for this kind of byplay."

"Biplane you mean."

"I've had a long, hard day at the office," she said, "and I'm bone-tired and all I want is a little peace and quiet, a chance to read the newspaper."

I'm writing these words a year later. We are getting ready to celebrate another birthday, Liam's twelfth. In his bedroom there is a model airplane that is still a jumble of sticks and thread and bits of plastic. When I have finished this, I will sit down with Liam and finish the plane and together we will launch it and together we will watch it crash into the pavement, as all the others have.

SIX

Corinne was in a bad mood. This is bad enough under any circumstances, even worse when I happen to be in a good mood. And I had been going through a small orgy of self-congratulation—who would have guessed that the family would be well fed from the beginning? And the meals, or so it seemed to me, were becoming nothing short of terrific.

There was no way to ignore Corinne's bad mood. The way I could determine that she was in a bad mood, and this is a generally infallible indication, was her unwavering refusal to exchange conversation with me. The fact that she was in a bad mood was indisputable; the mystery was *why*.

Possibly the mood was linked in some fashion to the vacuum-cleaner hose she was holding in her hand. Of course. She was vacuuming the living room, just as she had done before the great role switch.

"I don't want you doing that kind of work," I said to her. "Part of our deal was that you don't do any work around the house any more."

"But I can't stand it any longer."

"Can't stand what any longer?"

"I can't stand living this way any longer. Mike, I don't want to say anything . . ."

"You're already saying it."

"Well, I don't want to complain," she said. "I really don't. I know you're just starting out. But I can't go on living this way indefinitely. It clutters up my mind."

"I was going to get to the cleaning myself," I said. "Today as a matter of fact."

"But you've had two weeks and you haven't gotten to it," she said. "As long as I've got to live here, I don't want to live in a pigpen."

44

Harsh words. I looked around the living room and it seemed no worse than usual; better, in fact. But of course it had just been vacuumed and I couldn't take credit for that. I could feel my vision of myself as a successful homemaker start to dissolve, melted by the heat of Corinne's criticism.

"Well, maybe you haven't noticed it," I said, "but this is the way we've been living the past few years and I don't know why, all at once, you decide it's a pigpen. It'd be different if the house had ever been immaculate but . . ."

"Just a minute," she said. "I know that you never notice things like that, but I worked pretty hard to keep this house clean."

"Maybe you're beginning to think that this whole experiment is a mistake," I said. "Maybe you're starting to feel I should be back in an office."

This conversation, with variations, was replayed several times during the first weeks of the experiment and it had to be an indication of our doubts. But it always stopped there, the dare offered but not picked up.

What I did this time, by way of apology, was get the window-cleaning fluid and start polishing the panes in the living room. If Corinne noticed my efforts, she didn't find them worth mentioning. But then, she still wasn't finding much worth mentioning.

This would become our major problem. No two people ever reacted to their immediate environment in such different ways. The smallest vulgarities—a mass-produced front door, a print that has become too popular, a fake beam, a pastel-colored appliance—can propel Corinne into a dark mood. For some reason, possibly a single all-encompassing lack of taste, I am blind to these things. If there is a book to read or a television show to watch, I can do either quite happily in a cave. Corinne, on the other hand, would not be content living in a palace unless the color scheme was done properly.

Her attitude leads to much greater progress than does mine. It is her keen awareness of environment, her unwillingness to abide small flaws, that has led to the house's being constantly improved. The least I could do was keep the place clean. And immediately after our set-to, I began. All the furniture was moved out of the living room; the rugs were rolled up and taken out to air. I rubbed paste wax into the floors and buffed them; I shined the windows and decobwebbed the ceilings. And then I put everything back in place.

I'm sure that it must have looked better than when I began. But not all that much better. The work had eaten up two hours, two hours of boredom that fell somewhat short of exquisite. And then, as I watched in horror, the entire effect was undone by an eleven-year-old boy carrying a plate of crackers and the sports section of the newspaper.

I've since learned that cleaning a house is very much like ironing clothes—the first experience is dreadful and the second one, worse. These tasks require a numbness which, if one lacks at the outset, one soon tends to acquire. Acquiring numbness has never been one of my life goals. At times, even the simple mechanics of cleaning seemed beyond me. I've watched Corinne as she wades through a room, all motion and efficiency, and in my attempts to imitate her, I come out as kind of a slow-motion version, taking twice the time to accomplish half the work.

As I write these words, I have tried most of the housewifely chores, and my Achilles heel, my downfall, is clearly the ancient task of house cleaning. I am, I can only conclude, an incurable slob, and this is a fact that has, during my year as a housewife, caused not a little anquish.

On Valentine's Day, the waterbed developed a leak. This is a crisis that seems more modern than major, but I will say that it contributed precious little to any celebration in keeping with the traditions of Valentine's Day. Early—the alarm was at least an hour away from sounding—we extracted ourselves from a swamp of bedding and, looking like pups caught in a sudden rainstorm, made our way to the guest room and the old-fashioned unleakable bed we shared during the first years of marriage.

Sleep, once lost, was not soon found again. I was kept awake by presentiment of disaster. It is my experience that modern conveniences never perish alone; they always go in twos and threes. This is because all appliances are joined in a conspiracy and when one of them is injured it sends out a signal, inaudible to the human ear, that causes other appliances to develop sympathy pains. Thus, I was not at all surprised when both the dishwasher and the electric typewriter refused to start.

46

"I hate to leave for the office when everything is going wrong," Corinne said.

"You've got to go to work," I said.

But from the expression on her face—it was a smile—I felt that Corinne did not feel all that bad about going off to work, leaving me to cope with the emergencies. The appropriate repairmen were called and agreed to come over. However, there were no yellow-page listings for "waterbed service centers" and I suspected that was a problem I'd have to handle myself.

What had to be done was clear: all the water in the leaking polyethylene mattress—several hundred gallons of lukewarm, algae-infested water—had to be siphoned out through a garden hose running out the bedroom window and down a driveway. This would be a nuisance at any time of year, but in mid-February, with the hose coiled and frozen under several layers of snow, it qualified as something of a disaster. Corinne promised to bring a new hose home with her, and I set about cleaning the house between visits of repairmen.

The dishwasher man found that a fuse had been tripped ($13.40) and the IBM serviceman found a penny lodged in the mechanism ($21.40 plus mileage) and later in the day, the house straightened out, I went off to do the shopping. I returned at five o'clock to find the garden hose—but no sign of Corinne.

I walked slowly through the house that I had cleaned three hours earlier, just before the children came home from school. The three of them were at this moment parked in front of the three different television sets, each tuned to a different channel. They seemed to be in a state of rest; they were doubtless weary from the exertions required in ravaging an entire house.

Our youngest, Liam, was in the living room, watching cartoons, and on the cocktail table, beside the television set, were three books, the day's mail, photographs of the family, a used coffee cup, a pair of barber's shears, two magazines. The couch, its cushions freshly crumpled, was cluttered with newspapers and magazines; other newspapers, some yellowing at the edges, could be seen stacked beneath the couch. There was an open carton of oranges and grapefruit, a gift from relatives in Florida, left open in the middle of the floor. A portable typewriter uncovered on the toy chest. Random pieces of yellow copy paper on the floor. A chair left on its side. A sleeping dog, an electronic calculator, paper plates, grapefruit halves, spoons, sweaters, a peanut can filled with Popsicle sticks, several hundred baseball trading cards, an unplugged radio, a can of shoe polish, three political leaflets, tennis rackets.

In the kitchen, Siobhan, the thirteen-year-old, was watching a movie, something out of Barbara Stanwyck's blue period, and beyond her, in the laundry room, I could see the dozen towels left on the floor, right beside a paint roller, tray, and brushes—all splattered a vivid shade of yellow. Empty drinking glasses, a watering can, three telephone books, a half-dozen paper plates that had once held cat food and now served as swarming centers for ants, a bag of potatoes going to seed, tomato ends and onion peels left beside the cutting board, a pail of murky water with a sponge mop still standing upright in it, and a garbage can overflowing like some nightmarish horn of plenty.

Sean, the fourteen-year-old, was watching the nightly news show in his bedroom. To get there, I had to walk past the open door to Liam's bedroom. Recently we had built a closet for him, and I could see that he had not yet gotten the hang of it. The closet was still empty, beautifully clean and clear of clutter. The clothes had been left on the floor and draped over the bed. Also on the floor: a dozen game boards with all the pieces scattered, two flashlights, a shoeshine kit, dirty glasses. The bed did not merely look unmade; it seemed to have been the scene of some recent violent crime.

"This house is a shambles!" I announced over the video din. "What does all this mean? Two hours ago I left this house in terrific shape, spotless, as a matter of fact, and now it's a pigpen. It looks as though it was hit by a tornado."

One after another, the television sets were muted. I heard no response, but no response was required. My own words echoed in my mind, bringing back memories of my mother laying it on her three children. A shambles . . . a pigpen . . . hit by a tornado—I don't think I missed any of her pet phrases.

"Where's Mommy?" I asked.

"She went back to the office," Sean said.

"What do you mean she went back to the office? She wouldn't go back to the office just before dinner?"

"She wouldn't, huh?" Sean said. "Well, that's where she said you could call her when you were ready."

"Did she say anything else?"

"Nope," Sean said. "She just came in and looked around and then she left."

"She must have been pretty mad when she saw this place."

"I don't think so," he said. "She was laughing."

"Laughing? Well, I can tell you someone who is *not* laughing. Your father is not laughing. I want this house cleaned in twenty minutes. Starting now!"

I didn't add "or else" but I didn't have to; my tone of voice said it all. I remember this moment as a milestone. For the first time, or at least the first time I can remember, I was yelling at my three children. It's easy not to yell when you're not home to feel the brunt of the transgression. Maybe that was why Corinne was free to exit laughing: no longer was the mess her responsibility. At any rate, the yell had a certain novelty value and it seemed to work its magic on the kids. In record time they divided the house into three equal geographical areas and set to recleaning it.

And, as the debris was being cleared away, I prepared a special Valentine's Day dinner, veal in wine sauce. Corinne came in at seven to a clean house and a dinner cooking.

"I hope the condition of the house didn't bother you," I said.

"Oh no," she said. "I decided today that nothing would bother me. I just took one quick look at the house and went back to the office. It was much too nice a day to even think about a house like this and it does look much better now."

By dinnertime my mood had settled down somewhat. Corinne gave me a box of chocolates in commemoration of the day. In recent years I made a practice of presenting her with the largest, gaudiest, most ornate heart-shaped box to be found. And now the box that she was handing me was, well, box-shaped.

"Hmmm," I said, "I may not keep the cleanest house in the world, but I used to get you a larger box of candy."

"You know, I checked that out," she said. "What I found out was that you get about three times the amount of candy this way—with those other things you pay a fortune for a piece of ribbon."

"But, it's the romance of the . . ."

"And besides, I got you this," she said, handing me a single long-stemmed rose. "Happy Valentine's Day."

It worked. True, the house around us was always a mess, but this was a nice moment. And I took it to hand her my offering. In keeping with our reversed roles, I had gotten her a card this year, but no quiet understated or clever model for her. No, this was the fifty-cent card, lavish and large, bright red with a row of silver hearts along the border, positively dripping sentiment. Corinne picked it up tentatively, read the verse I had chosen for her, and clasped it to her bosom.

I have a man, a wonderful man,
Who gives meaning to my life—
Who makes me feel loved and wanted
And proud to be his wife!

Who fills my days with happiness
And warms my heart with love.
The wonderful man is you, the one
I think the whole world of!

Visitors. Corinne's closest friend, Stella Schwartz, brought her mother over for a little visit in March. This time I went all out—fresh home-made bread, tea, pleasant conversation. And I couldn't help but feel good when I heard Stella's mother talking to Corinne.

"Isn't it wonderful, the things he does around the house," she said. "The bread was wonderful and the tea was very nice. And he does all the ironing too? And to think he stays home all day while you go to work—what a nice man he is!"

I couldn't help it; there was a warm glow that lasted until I escorted the two women to the front door and bade them farewell.

"One thing though," Stella's mother said as they left, "he's not much of a house cleaner."

My inability to clean house kept coming back to bother me like some recurring ailment, and as nearly as I could tell, it was incurable. To most people, cleanliness is next to godliness—to me, it's next to impossible.

The reason is simple. There is no way for me to put my heart into the job. In my time I have done most of the dumb jobs that people put on book jackets—I've been a landscape gardener, a house painter, a forest-service lookout, a caddie, a waiter—and I've always been able to do this work because it seemed to free my mind for other, more important matters. While painting a house, one can outline a novel, chart a future, dream a dream.

But I was never able to approach house cleaning the same way, possibly because the cleaning jobs are numerous and diverse. There is not enough sameness to free your mind for other thoughts. Consequently you devote your mind to the tasks at hand, hosing down screens, scrubbing sinks, and what-not.

And the job had to be done. My inadequacies had gotten to Corinne and were proving debilitating. On the first Sunday of April, I walked into the kitchen and found her bent over the table, her head in her arms. She may have been crying; I didn't want to ask.

"You don't understand!" It came out in short deadly bursts. "It doesn't matter to you that we live in a pigpen. But I just can't think clearly. Not with everything cluttered like this. I've finally got the feeling there is nowhere I can go. My house is awful. You know what I do some days? I just go out and sit in the car."

Corinne was gathering momentum when the phone rang. It was her parents, making their weekly telephone call from their retirement home in Florida. I watched Corinne struggle against her black mood and finally overcome it. No matter how things are falling down around her, she has never shared her troubles. And of course she would never admit to her parents that she had made a less-than-perfect catch. But how often can I be saved by the bell?

It happened again, another bleak mood. It was income-tax day but this year it can't be blamed on the income tax. The tax had been settled some weeks earlier, and I was beginning to feel chipper about the whole thing. This coming year, if everything went according to plan, I would make absolutely no money. And while poverty has never been one of the great personal goals in my life, I received enormous pleasure just imagining the act of filling out my tax returns for the current year.

51

"I've got to get moving," Corinne said after dinner. "I've been delaying everything much too long. I should have had the new brochure out months ago."

The brochure was to include the new products that seemed so promising—a breadbox she was importing from Denmark, a new aerosol plastic cleaner. Sitting down beside her, I went over the wording for the new brochure. However, none of my offerings seemed quite right to Corinne. Was I losing my touch?

"And just look at this house!" she suddenly said. "This house is such a mess. We've just got to come up with a new system before I go crazy."

"I'm sorry," I said. "I've got to admit that's the one thing I haven't been able to muster up any enthusiasm for."

"But no one can," she said. "I never heard of anyone any-where—outside of some very sick people—who ever mustered up any enthusiasm for cleaning a house. That shouldn't matter. The cooking is easy—to tell you the truth, I was even a little jealous when you took over the cooking. No one likes to do the cleaning. But someone has got to."

"Easy," I said. "Just because your work isn't going well is no reason to take it out on me. You used to tell me something—try and leave the work at the office—and that's not a bad idea."

"It isn't the work," she said. "That's not what's bothering me. I can handle my work, my end of the bargain. It's just that this place is a shipwreck."

The way one can tell that Corinne is close to losing her temper, she speaks extra evenly, and at this point her voice had become a monotone. There was more discussion along the same line, none of it worth recording, but the outcome was that I tried harder to do a better job with the cleaning. Day after day I waited for every-one to leave and I plugged in the vacuum cleaner and listened to a whine that has always struck me about as pleasant as the noise a fingernail makes on a blackboard. Then the thinking would begin. I would think: this house is plenty clean enough. I would think: what's she complaining about anyway? And I would think: what surprises me, in fact, is just how clean it is—yes, it happens to be *very* clean. And then I would think: besides, it's almost time to start preparing dinner.

Well, almost time. First I would switch on the television set and talk to the dog and open a book and check the mail and read two newspapers and heat up the coffee and grab a catnap and by then, well, it was almost time to start preparing dinner.

In early June, Corinne clipped a story from the New York *Times*. It was about couples who are learning to share household chores. It seemed that most of the men did the housework while most of the women did the cooking.

One paragraph in the news story had been circled in red: "When Marian Anderson, an executive with Van Raalte, who works in Manhattan, comes home at night, she frequently finds that her husband, Fred, has vacuumed the house and polished the furniture . . ."

"What do you think of that?" Corinne said. "He *likes* it."

"Fink."

Failure was mine. The extent of my failure, just what it had meant to my wife, was explained to me that day. Every Wednesday night I played basketball with other aging athletes and the night before I had been out on the courts. The game was generally followed by a few drinks and some mild socializing.

"Don't you ever wonder what I'm doing on Wednesday nights?" Corinne asked me.

"You've been doing something Wednesday nights?"

"Not that you'd notice," she said. "But while you've been out playing basketball, I've been cleaning this house from one end to the other."

"You have?"

"I had to, to preserve my sanity. But I'm tired of doing it every Wednesday. One reason I agreed to trade roles with you was I didn't want to do that any more."

"You should have told me," I said. "I had no idea."

"I didn't want you to know," she said. "In fact, those first few weeks I would clean the house and then take some things out and leave them scattered around. Newspapers, dirty clothes, coats. Just so you wouldn't know what I had been doing. Later I thought the hell with that, I wouldn't leave anything around, but you still haven't noticed."

Guilt built. I could see only two possible solutions to the house-cleaning problem. One was to apply myself more diligently, master all the mechanics and do several hours of work a day. The other possible solution was to hire a cleaning woman.

I called Norman, a regular at the Pier Three.

"Norman, are you still using a cleaning woman?"

"A cleaning *girl,*" he told me. "Yeah, she's only twenty-one years old and she does a hell of a job."

"Could I have her number?"

"Sure, I'll get it for you," he said. "Let me tell you the story. She hits you for three dollars an hour but she supplies her own transportation. Last I heard, she still had two free days every week. And she's got small tits."

"Small tits?"

"Just thought you'd like to know."

"Norman, I couldn't care less." Ah, the loftiness that comes with liberation. "How're her shoulders?"

"Well, there is one other thing," Norman said. "She won't clean the oven."

"I don't blame her," I said. "I didn't even know you were supposed to clean the oven."

By summertime the problem was solved, at least partially solved, by enlisting the aid of a young woman who came in one day a week to clean everything but the oven.

I still felt some guilt; once again I had failed to accomplish a task that millions of people accept as their lot of life. But the house was given a semblance of order at least once a week and that order generally lasted approximately three days and that fact freed our life of crisis for at least a half week at a time.

To be entirely honest about this thing, I am not at all sure that my failing is one of character. In fact, I am beginning to think that Corinne may be coming around to my way of thinking. With the regular arrival of the professional cleaning woman, she stopped picking up everything that was out of place and one day toward the end of the year I noticed a fine layer of dust had gathered on the vacuum cleaner.

"You've taught me one thing," she said. "I've seen how hard it is for you to do the dumb jobs—and that's because you've never

54

had to do them; you've never gotten into the habit. I've decided I'm never going to waste another hour doing the dirty work around here. I spent fifteen years doing the dumbest jobs imaginable and no one ever even noticed. Never again."

SEVEN

Sometimes there is just no way to escape the male role, the male world, the male reactions. I had threatened to take Siobhan to Mother-Daughter night at the school, and only her sincere entreaties saved us from that experience. So it was, instead, Father-Son night with Liam at his school.

In years past I had worked late or caught a convenient cold or just simply begged off. Never mind, there were always guilt pangs, and this year there would be no excuse, no easy out. Earlier in the week Liam had come home with the news that there would be some hockey players on hand for Father-Son night, hockey players attached to a local minor-league team called the Ducks.

"Maybe they'll show a movie," Liam said, "a movie of their best games."

"It would be a short movie." I've always been a close reader of the sports pages. But why this unseemly resistance? Whatever the reason, a kind of edginess built during the day. After supper, I took the trouble to shave a second time. Then I debated whether to wear a tie or not. Every time I make an excursion into their world, the children's world, I worry about the costuming.

This was Liam's world—a grade-school cafeteria lit by four long overhead strips of fluorescence. The cement-block walls, painted institutional green, were decorated with youthfully impressionistic paintings and "No Smoking" signs.

The five hockey players, unfamiliar representatives of an unfamiliar sport, were standing at the front of the room. Hockey does not, in this temperate clime, have the same sure appeal of baseball or football but it is a game, and that is the important thing. The strongest links between generations are the games, and these

55

players were situated in age midway between the fathers and the sons.

"I'd like to tell all of you kids to get your education so that you'll always have something to fall back on," the first player said. "And another thing is you really have to have the desire to play; you really have to *want* to play."

These were evidently sound points because they were repeated nearly verbatim by each of the five players. Possibly they are to be found in a speaking kit given to all professional athletes attending these events, a programed part of the ritual. And it was most definitely a ritual. Although the cafeteria was filled to capacity, the atmosphere remained formal, contained. There was the intense politeness of the village males listening to campfire tales told by visiting warriors.

There were questions to be asked, and earlier in the day Liam had gotten at least one question firmly in mind—why did the goalies have larger sticks than any of the other players? Other sons had other questions, many of them having to do with the hockey sticks.

"What kind of wood do you use?" one player was asked.

"There are several different kinds," he said. "Ash is popular and some of the sticks are laminated. The goalie's stick is made a little stronger than a player's stick because he has to stop all those shots."

The flow of information remained formal, functional, easily digested by both fathers and sons. We learned of the type of tape used on the sticks, the weight of the puck, the speed of a skater, the value of talcum powder on the hands, the amount of money earned by top pros, the dangers of the game.

"Oh, I've had my nose broken," an apparently unmarked young player was saying. "Many players get their noses broken one or two times a year. I've had cuts over my eyes, loose teeth—oh, I've had a few real bruises myself."

The player was asked whether people in the audience ever get hit by flying pucks.

"Girls," he said. "Sometimes a girl won't be paying any attention to the game and she'll get hit—but that's typical of the female race."

The remark, pure in its male chauvinism, got laughter and

56

applause from the assembled males. This year, however, my reactions were changing and the laugh didn't come. Then it was time for refreshment. The men, each separated by a boy who had not yet reached a third of his growth, stood for long moments waiting to choose among nine varieties of cookies and paper cups filled with vermillion and orange liquids.

"Boys, please take only two cookies."

The dietician was young, unexpectedly chic, and I was immediately ashamed of having noticed these facts. Liam, however, was too busy violating the two-cookie restriction to be aware of such things.

During the eating of the cookies, there was some mingling, some talk—always of games and game playing. I studied the other men carefully. Were they younger, better dressed, more successful, more in tune with their offspring? Should I have worn the damn tie? Liam seemed to suffer from no such self-doubts; he was too busy dissolving his cookies in his soft drink.

And then it was over. In twos—bears and cubs—the males went out into the moonlit night, the fathers finally loosening their collars and throwing their arms around the boys, the sons starting to laugh and talk rapidly, everyone relaxed, the ordeal behind them.

EIGHT

A house is not a home; it's a prison. A least that's what it can become when you're confined to it, day and night, for weeks and months at a time. For the first time in many years I was doing without an office, living a single-structure existence, and the walls had closed in on me.

And then Corinne realized one of the great American dreams, the dream just a notch below the one that has you being discovered at a Hollywood soda fountain. A magazine decided to do a picture spread on our home. *Our* home! The color magazine attached to the New York *Sunday News,* the most widely circulated paper in the country, had picked our home for one of those lavish color spreads. And we realized then that no matter what had happened to our individual dreams of glory along life's highway, at least our house had arrived.

It had been a long uphill struggle for Home Sweet Home, and when I heard the news from Corinne, I couldn't help but think back to its humble beginnings in 1960. The price then had been $16,500, which is what people used to pay for a nice little home in the suburbs. It was then about the proper size to qualify for bungalowhood, one of those die-cut little semi-ranches scarcely large enough to support a pretension. It was a home built with areas instead of rooms—a kitchen area, a dining area, a living area, not much more.

But that didn't matter, not then. Ours was the first home built on a huge Long Island estate that had just been broken up and sold to developers and we were, those first few months, alone in a rich man's woodland, surrounded by raccoons and ring-necked pheasants and in the garden we would dig up an occasional arrowhead. And then the developers moved in around us and the next few years we awakened to the sound of trees crashing and huge bulldozers scraping hills flat and when it was over, when the developers had turned greenery into folding green, we were surrounded by and overshadowed by huge, boxy, asphalt-shingle-sided monsters from some primitive era. Jimmy Durante has a phrase for it: "What a revoltin' development."

Our family grew and filled the small home, finally driving me away from the bedroom typewriter and out in search of gainful employment at the nearest newspaper. The house grew to accommodate the family. The carport became a garage one year and a master bedroom the next. Wings sprouted on either side of the house, one wing larger than the original house had been—a wing that Corinne designed with sleeping loft and window walls and beams and cathedral ceilings.

The original "living area" became a supermodern kitchen; the original "kitchen area" and "dining area" combined to form a barely adequate laundry room. And now we had come to a time when we were scarcely able to trace the outlines of the original home.

It has been a good home, a comfortable home, and—because

Corinne has always been a frustrated architect—a dramatic home. If in the nineteen-fifties girls had been told that it was possible to become an architect, the plastics world would have lost one of its designer-manufacturers. At any rate, the house became her clay during the first, often frustrating, decade of marriage, and I, for one, was not in the least surprised when the *Sunday News* decided that it was worth several pages of color pictures. Corinne, however, reacted in the manner of a beginning actress walking accidentally onto stage and receiving a rousing round of applause; she was surprised.

"Don't worry," I told her. "This time I'll really do a cleaning job."

"Don't *you* worry," she said to me.

Her reaction seemed strangely relaxed. I had been thinking this would be a good opportunity to make amends, to put everything else aside and give the cleaning my best shot. However, Corinne did not trust me. So, two days before the arrival of a photographer representing the largest newspaper in the country, I came home to find a strange woman polishing the windows and waxing the floors.

"Don't walk across *my* floors," she yelled at me. "Can't you see they're still wet?"

The woman was doing more than just cleaning. She was, for example, taking apart the range knobs and soaking them in an ammonia solution. I had never known that the knobs came off.

"Don't leave nothing laying around!" she yelled at me. "I've got better things to do than pick up after you."

The house quickly became almost *too* clean; suddenly, I didn't feel comfortable in my own home. I realized then that I had been suffering under a misapprehension. I had assumed that the *News* was sending a photographer to take pictures of our house because they wanted pictures of the house we lived in. That, however, was far from the truth. After the designer-author had selected our house, after that decision had been approved by the appropriate editors, then the house was changed.

Originally it was the lived-in home of a beer-drinking, tabloid-reading, game-playing, slightly sloppy suburbanite. What it became, in time, was the home of a horticulturally-minded, art-loving, wine-sipping connoisseur of the good life. It started out with its own personality and it became very much like all those other homes that magazines decide to photograph. It struck me just a little like changing the rules after the game had begun.

At first I found it funny, then just slightly enraging. Suddenly I had become invisible, the non-essential person. Corinne dropped everything—her business, her interests, her friends—and spent every moment cleaning places and things that had never felt the feathery touch of a dustcloth before.

The first thing I noticed was the amazing disappearance of most of my prized possessions. It was as though a selective thief—say, a cat burglar with questionable taste—was coming in at night and whisking away only those objects that I liked.

An example. During the past half-dozen years, one wall in the living room had been decorated by eight Toulouse-Lautrec prints. I had not selected them, but I had become accustomed to living with them; they had, in fact, become old friends, and in the evenings, while sitting on the sofa reading the newspaper, I would frequently rest my eyes by glancing up above the paper and studying them. They were not his most popular works, but they were among his most interesting. One night, resting my eyes, I looked up and saw, instead of my friends, eight slightly dark rectangles, spaces that had not been faded by the sun's rays because, until then, they had been covered by pictures.

"Where are the paintings?"

"I've been meaning to get rid of them for years," Corinne said. "Now was a good time."

I returned to my newspaper. By this time I know better than to argue with my wife on any matter of taste. There is a logical reason for this; her taste is so much better than my own. ("How can you be sure about that?" she once asked me. "Look who we married," she was told.) I had, for example, clung to a reproduction of an Andrew Wyeth painting long after it had passed from fashion and was being dismissed as a superb example of collegiate sentimentality. Corinne not only knows the precise moment to jettison such things, to alter taste, but she is usually a jump ahead of everyone else. Similarly, my theories of home decoration seem to leave something to be desired. I would start any basic scheme with a La-Z-Boy reclina-rocker in naugahyde.

The Toulouse-Lautrecs were just the beginning. Boxes of spices and random cereals suddenly disappeared from the kitchen shelves, to be replaced by rows of delicate long-stemmed wine glasses. Next went the vinegar bottles, the crackers, all the pots and pans without copper bottoms, the old toy chests, two chairs, any antiques. My well-stocked plastic bar, all magazines and newspapers. Gone from the front hallway was the hundred-pound bag of lime, twenty pounds of sand, some cement—and these had been there so long I no longer knew their intended use. Gone, too, a toy printing press that had been sighted in various spots throughout the house since Christmas 1972. A bowling bag and ball, the winter coats, the tennis rackets, the golf clubs, the pool cue. One day they were there where they had always been, the next day they were gone without a trace. Many of the objects reappeared weeks and months later in the bottom of kitchen cupboards and in the basement and in the tool shed. Some have never been found.

The house began to seem . . . empty. Where were the baskets of laundry, the kitchen garbage receptacle, the empty grocery bags, the cartons from the liquor store, the fishing pole, the other signs of a dissolute, fun-filled existence?

The vanished objects were replaced by other things, props that did not speak of dissolution or fun but rather of taste and sophistication. Two days before the arrival of the photographer—The Photographer, as he loomed in our minds—there appeared, stretched the length of the living-room wall, a deep crimson Navaho rug. There was something familiar about that rug. After studying it for a few moments, I realized that it was no stranger. It had, in fact, been in the house before, though briefly, a year earlier. Corinne had brought it home from a dealer to ask my opinion of it.

"It depends on the price," I had said.

"What do you mean by that?"

"Well, if it were under fifty dollars, I'd love it," I explained. "If it were under eighty dollars, I'd like it quite a lot. How much is it anyway?"

"You're going to *hate* this rug," she had said.

Actually, when I learned the price, my reaction went beyond hatred to scorn. The price had been close to five hundred dollars and that struck me as a lot to pay for a rug you couldn't walk on.

61

But this year I had not been consulted. After all, it was not *my* five hundred dollars; it was Corinne's—and so was the decision.

It was the beginning of a priceless collection of hanging rugs, a collection that was to be ours for the entire day that The Photographer spent in our home. A neighbor and friend, Mary Ann Mauro, is one of the country's outstanding weavers and she showed up one morning with hangings that were colorful and dramatic and added just the right touch of warmth to the basically modern decor. They were just the kind of things we would love to have—if we could ever afford them. But this is something that the readers of the *News* will never know, because the hangings were quickly draped over every conceivable surface of the house.

At the same time, exotic house plants suddenly sprouted from all the least likely places. High on the kitchen beams, beyond the reach of humans, in a spot where they could be seen but not watered, was a small garden of asparagus ferns. One could stumble over vases, planters, and hanging plants in every room of the house. It was possible to come down with hay fever by simply walking from one room to another.

No longer was it the home of fairly typical suburbanites, the kind of people who could relax in the company of Toulouse-Lautrec prints. Suddenly there was room for pretensions. What it was becoming, hour by hour, was all those other homes photographed in all those other magazines, all those homes that people study with envy and then say, in hushed tones, "It looks like no one lives there." What an accolade!

Now at least I understand why they are so clean, so shining, so tasteful. It is because everyone who has a home photographed is nervous and thrilled and anxious to have a home that looks like all those other homes in all those other photographs.

Me, I just watched. It was a pleasure *not* to be part of the process. Most of the truly effective props were supplied by the writer of the story, a gifted decorator named Elaine Salkaln. She brought food, for example. Oh, not that we didn't have food. When you have five people living together, it is essential that you have some food. It's just that the food we had on hand wasn't photogenic enough. Elaine opened the refrigerator door and her eyes took in the half-eaten yoghurts, the limp carrots, the cheeses encrusted with mold, the parsley that was losing its color, the containers filled with leftovers.

"I'll clean that up," I said nervously, but Ms. Salkaln seemed not to hear. "Believe me, it'll be okay by the time The Photographer gets here."

I opened the pantry door, and the usual array of products—tinned tomato sauces, dog food, napkins—came tumbling out. Ms. Salkaln said nothing, but I sensed that our food was failing some vital test.

Ms. Salkaln was a model of efficiency. That same day she brought over some bread—not just your basic loaf of Pepperidge Farm bread. No, she had gone to a special bakery, possibly one that catered to the needs of interior decorators and she brought a long loaf that would look splendid in Corinne's newest product, the see-through breadbox. And she also brought some circular loaves of bread that she looped on pegs above the kitchen table.

"What're they?" I asked.

"Just loaves of bread," Corinne said. "We can eat them—I know you think they're phony, but we'll eat them as soon as The Photographer goes."

As I write these words, many months after the fact, the circles of bread are still looped over the pegs and idle visitors could not be faulted for wondering whether some bakers had come in for a big ring-toss tournament. Still, I don't feel qualified to question anyone on matters of taste and every so often I do my bit by dusting them off. They are now hard enough so that I could scrub them down, if that were necessary, and perhaps some day I will give them a coat of shellac.

Ms. Salkaln had also found, through visiting specialty shops as far as fifteen miles away, a perfect bunch of radishes and, at another store, an extremely picturesque bunch of carrots. These two items were left—casually, you understand—in a prominent spot just above the kitchen sink.

"Well," Corinne told me, "I might have put them in that spot."

"There?"

"Well, maybe for a few minutes."

In a large clear glass bowl were left such seemingly disparate objects as oranges and artichokes. The lemons were left, for some reason, in a hanging wire basket above the kitchen work surface. I liked that so much that I still keep lemons there today. In still another large bowl, Elaine started to construct a photogenic salad. However, she had only enough lettuce to make a small salad and so, unbeknownst to me, she filled the bottom of the bowl with space-filling objects, grapefruits and artichokes, and then she scattered the lettuce leaves over them. This was all well and good, a first-rate imitation salad, and would have photographed very well, I'm sure, except for the fact that The Photographer wanted to get a picture of me tossing the salad and what he got was a picture of me tossing a grapefruit up into the air.

That sort of set the tone for realism. Everywhere I looked I saw wine glasses, enough to put a small glassware shop in business. Scattered over our rug, the only rug in the house that we owned, were huge pillows I had never seen before. They were the kind of pillows that models in *Vogue* magazine are always sitting down upon. The trouble with them is that most of the people we know are relatively unsophisticated and still sit in chairs.

There was one completely practical touch and I will take full credit for that; it was my sole contribution. In every room could be seen, prominently displayed, a full array of Corinne's latest products.

Ms. Salkaln took care of the other details. I noticed that even the books in the bookcases had been, well, rearranged. There are several hundred books there, and suddenly the books at the ends of the shelves were the ones with the most colorful jackets. The only titles that would appear in the photographs were either extremely photogenic (*Marilyn* by Mailer) or reasonably hip (*Breakfast of Champions* by Vonnegut) or out-and-out classics (*The Collected Works of Shakespeare*).

The house was, finally, perfect. By that I mean it had been transformed into the kind of place no one would want to live in, and it was, needless to say, important to keep it that way. ("I don't want anyone to go into the living room," I heard. "Do you have to sit there?" I heard. "Out!" I heard.)

Entering the house was like walking into a slow gleam. It was not that the house had never been this clean before; I was confidant that *no* house had ever been this clean before. The rooms that had been cleaned were, I might add, the rooms that The Photographer might conceivably want to photograph. The

64

other rooms—the children's bedrooms, the second bathroom, the laundry room—were left the way they usually were. This led to an experience right out of the old "Twilight Zone"—walking from an immaculate and modern room, turning a corner, finding yourself in a slum.

At last, the big day! I knew early in the morning that this was the day of The Photographer because of the sudden appearance of bouquets of fresh flowers and baskets of fruit selected for plumpness. I was feeling less relevant than I ever had in my life and when Corinne started to study me critically—should she send out for a younger, leaner model?—I took the opportunity to join the Toulouse-Lautrec prints and disappear.

At noon, when I called in, I was instructed to bring home food and drink for the Photographer. I picked up a cold six-pack and a bagful of heroes. It was the proper selection. The Photographer shared a certain quality with all the other newspaper photographers I've known, a kind of regular-guy distillate, and I didn't have to be told what was going on in his mind as he wandered through this . . . this museum.

I noticed that Corinne was as buffed and polished as the house itself. She was, at this moment, wearing a long dress, and a smile that would brighten any newspaper supplement. When I came home she was sitting at the dining-room table, which had been covered with a bold new Marimekko fabric, and in front of her, on the table, on the fabric, was a huge, new, never used table-model power saw.

"Don't ask," she said.

I didn't have to. I had been witness to, and participant in, enough staged photographs in my life to guess at the story line: big-time plastics manufacturer at work at home. The Photographer looked me over, sized me up, seemed to sense that I didn't fit in with anything as glamorous as this house or this wife, and went on with his work. I sat there, mumbling about the sandwiches and beer, but the only one to notice me was Ms. Salkaln.

"Oh, no beer," the decorator said. "Today we're drinking wine."

She had poured us each a nice goblet of red wine. I'm sure that it was very nice, and would look especially nice in any pho-

tograph, but at that point I had a desperate desire to escape what
had once been my home.

"I've got to go," I said to Corinne.

"Oh, don't go," she said. "The Photographer wants to put you
in some pictures later on."

Too late. I had, in truth, made an appointment with the dentist
for early afternoon.

"I've got to have that root-canal work done today," I said.

"I never saw anyone so happy to have root-canal work done,"
Corinne said.

"Oh yes," I said. "And there's one other little thing I have to
do."

"What's that?"

"I want to rent a new dog," I said, looking at Lester. "The one
they sent over this morning needs a haircut."

"Get out of here," she said.

The Photographer looked up at that one. Well, I finally got his
attention. I whistled all the way to the dentist's office and never
have I been so happy in my pain. I would have stayed there the
entire afternoon, or at least as long as The Photographer was oc-
cupying the house, but he ran out of things to do to me and I had
to go home.

When I got home in midafternoon, he was still there. The kids
were just coming in from the school bus and there was a noticea-
ble hush as they came into the house, as they walked from the
sunlight into a . . . mausoleum. They walked past their mother
and The Photographer, walked past all this beauty into their bedrooms, and the silence was shattered by the voice of a thirteen-
year-old girl ringing through the house.

"WHO PUT ALL THIS CRAP IN MY ROOM?"

"Don't say crap," I shouted back at her.

I went to her room, and I must admit it was difficult to get into
the door of her room. The small room was filled with coats that
used to hang in the hall, paintings that used to hang on the wall,
and a thousand other objects that some higher authority had
decided to conceal in her room. Siobhan had been quite accurate;
her room was filled with crap.

"Look, kids," I said, "it's all going to end soon. Now I want you

66

to get cleaned up so that The Photographer can take your picture."

"Not me," said Sean.

"I'm not going to be in any picture," Siobhan said.

"Me neither," said Liam.

"I wasn't asking you," I said. "I was telling you. Now this is very important to your mother and I want you kids scrubbed."

They had my sympathy but not my support. It's next to impossible to get them to sit still when their grandfather is taking their pictures, and persuading them to pose for a total stranger was no easier. I suspected they would get even, but I didn't know what method they would select. Then I saw Siobhan leading The Photographer to Liam's bedroom.

"Why don't you take some pictures of this room?" the girl was saying. "It's really very nice."

The Photographer looked in quickly, then looked away. The dirty socks, the blankets left on the floor, a dead goldfish floating on top of the tank, the scattered games. I could see The Photographer was interested.

"Can I help you?"

"Yes." He changed his mind. "Actually, I'd like to get a picture of you and your wife eating."

"Fine," I said. "Let me go and get the caviar."

"Caviar-really?"

"No," I said.

By this time I was counting the minutes. How much longer could this go on? As The Photographer was looking anxiously at the sun descending toward the horizon, I was looking at that same sun and rooting it on.

"Didn't you want to take some more pictures of Mike?" Corinne asked.

"Yes, I did," The Photographer said.

Were they just being polite? Was this some con to make me feel part of the story? Well, I could play the role as well as the next fellow. I went to the bedroom closet, to the back of the closet, and found a white safari jacket I had bought one summer in a moment of whimsy and never had the guts to wear. Somehow this seemed the right moment for a safari jacket.

"Oh, I suppose you think that's funny," Corinne said.

"Where's my ascot?" I said to her. "I've been looking everywhere and I can't find my ascot."

The Photographer took a couple of pictures, possibly just to be polite, and quickly lost interest in me. Splendid. I saw him photographing Corinne with some of her latest products and I snuck out to the backyard hammock where I promptly fell asleep. I woke up hearing the click of a camera shutter; it was twilight and The Photographer was less than two feet from my face, clicking away. Finally, the sun did set and The Photographer left and Corinne spent the next three days in bed with a low-grade fever and headaches, recovering.

In time we managed to replace the fuses blown by the photographer's lights. Mary Ann Mauro came and took back her weavings. The flowers wilted and the potted plants disappeared and the wax stopped its infernal shining. I found the cooking utensils, the spices, the storage chests, the fireplace screen. We're still missing some things—there's an egg beater I'd love to find—but at the end of the week I came in and there were mud tracks all over the living room and the bag of cement was back in the hallway and for the first time all week, I could breathe easy. Everything was going to be all right.

NINE

"God!" Corinne was making a face. "What mixture do you use in the coffee?"

"The usual," I said. "The same as we've always used—is something wrong?"

"Just the taste," she said.

"I thought it tasted pretty good."

"Well, it's terrible." She was relentless. "Maybe I should get one of those one-cup coffee makers, then I could make my own coffee in the office."

And then she went off. What upset me most was not the coffee, or even the criticism of the coffee, but my reaction to that criticism. I have started taking these things to heart. Gradually I am turning into the woebegone bride in the Maxwell House commercials, the one who gets the coffee instructions from Cora in the general store. Can't I do anything right?

TEN

I have never enjoyed going out. During recent years I have avoided dinner invitations as though my plate-mates were known carriers of social diseases. If there is any such thing as personal purgatories, mine will surely resemble one of those chummy little suburban parties where neighbors gather in circles, gently massaging one another's ego as weariness and booze do battle for the senses.

It may well be that my anti-social attitude was an occupational hazard. The job of column writing is never quite so glamorous as others imagine, but it does tend to get one out and about. I had in recent years been able to see all the plays, the fights, the games, the premieres, and the parties.

Before too many weeks as a househusband, I began to feel new urges, prominent among them the desire to go out. Out where? It didn't matter. Out why? I had no idea. I did know, however, that the urge was accompanied by the awakening of another feeling that was new to me. A feeling of depression. I'm not here talking about a blue Monday or a small snit or a downer—but, rather, a bona fide, bone-deep blueness capable of coloring my life for days at a time.

Anything could set me off. It might be a shopping trip, a money problem, a dinner gone bad, a combination of factors. It hit me for the first time one day in February. I was staying home, watching dough rise, and I knew there was still a sizable shopping to do. I was running short of both time and money, and there seemed no way to reach the bank by its closing hour. I called Corinne and asked her whether she would mind walking downstairs to the bank beside her office and cashing a check for me.

"I'm really quite busy," she said over the phone.

"Fine," I said, "and the chances are excellent that the kids are going to be really quite hungry."

"Oh, all right," she said.

I sensed that Corinne was, at that moment, involved in one business crisis or another. Still, her reaction left me with a feeling of helplessness. And as I remained home waiting for the dough to rise a second time, I could feel the bile rising simultaneously. Why am I doing this? What kind of a simp job is this? Why the hell don't I just chuck this and go back and work for a living?

Rather than race into town for the money and the last-minute shopping, I decided to make do with what was on hand. I would transform last night's stew into a hearty soup, add a chef's salad and bread hot from the oven. The projected menu sounded good to me—simple but good. I wouldn't try to explain it, I'd just serve it. The real trouble didn't begin until the family was gathered at the table.

"What's for dinner?" Sean said.

"We're trying something a little different tonight," I said. "Fresh baked bread, beef soup, and a big Caesar salad."

"What's the meat?"

"Where is it written that you must have meat every night?"

"No meat?" Sean stared at me disbelievingly. "You're actually being serious and you're actually not giving us any meat tonight?"

"You're kidding," Siobhan said.

I had a powerful but temporary urge to toss the dinner at those assembled. The event thereafter proceeded in silence. Sean, deciding to punish me for my failure, went very light on both the soup and the salad and decided not to try the bread at all. The high spot was provided by Liam.

"Wow, this bread is great!" he said.

"Well, thanks . . ."

"It tastes just like store bread," he completed the compliment.

"Liam, come over here where I can hit you."

"What's the matter, dear?" Corinne said. "Did you have a rough day?"

"Well, I had a lot of trouble finding someone who would cash a check for me."

"I was really busy then," she said. "It just came at the wrong time, that's all. I've got an idea—why don't I take you to a movie?"

"We went last night."

"That doesn't matter," she said. "We can go again if it'll cheer you up."

"It's okay," I said.

Corinne seemed relieved not to have to go out to another movie. This gave her the opportunity to retire to the living room with a briefcase full of invoices and bills; every night now she was taking work home and this fact served to add fuel to my depression. But why was this bad mood different than past bad moods? It was different in strength, depth, and duration—a migraine of a mood. What distinguished it, also, was my powerlessness against it. If I could have isolated a specific cause, I might have been able to find a specific solution. But there was a lack of definition, an absence of an edge.

"Oh," Corinne called to me, "I arranged for us to go to the premiere of *The Great Gatsby* next week. We'll go with Lou and Stella. You'll like that."

The premiere was something to look forward to. It had come to that; I was anticipating the celebrity-studded preview of a bad movie. It was enough that we would be eating out and I would have a night off.

Before joining our friends Lou and Stella at the restaurant, I made a vague excuse and wandered off on my own. It was my first visit to the city in many weeks, and I wanted the chance just to walk up and down the streets of Manhattan. The pimps were at their gaudiest, the hookers at their most glamorous, and I wandered down this midway blinking at the lights, as wide-eyed as any other hick.

Finally, there was a sufficiency and I joined the others at a new, much praised Chinese restaurant. The food seemed superb, although I must admit that I seemed to overreact to any dinner that someone else cooked. At the end of the meal, Corinne came up with her credit card and suggested to Lou that they split the bill. Lou, a gentleman to the core, seemed vaguely embarrassed by that thought and countered by proposing he pick up the whole tab.

71

While they were fighting over the pleasure of paying, Corinne suddenly noticed something.

"How come yours is golden?"

"What?"

"Your credit card," she said, "how come it's golden and mine is green?"

"It's an executive credit card," he said.

"Well, why didn't they give me one of those? I'll bet they don't even allow women to have golden credit cards."

"Hey," I said, "mine is green."

"Let me see it."

Corinne was not satisfied until I produced a card that matched her own. She seemed convinced then that it was not a part of the plot against womankind. However, I know in my heart that one day she will ask for one of those golden cards, just to be sure.

Corinne had handled the battle of the bill perfectly and it wound up being divided. The only thing she had trouble with, and it was a source of trouble throughout the year, was figuring out the proper amount to tip.

"How much is it?" she whispered.

"Whatever Lou decides," I whispered back.

It was nice to be out, nice not to have to cook the meal, nice to have someone else buying the meal, nice to sit through a movie, even an enormous turkey like *The Great Gatsby*. And what was particularly nice was to run into Clay Felker, the publisher of *New York* magazine, on the way out of the theater.

"I thought we were going to get together," he said. "I thought we were going to have a lunch and talk over some article ideas."

"That sounds good to me."

"Well, then, let's do it," he said. "Let's have that lunch next week."

"Sure," I said. "I'll do that."

I almost licked his hand out of sheer gratitude. The world of *New York* magazine—a world of hip, beautiful, with-it people—has never been my world exactly but I can't describe the feeling of being wanted after a few months of not even being noticed.

Several months later when we were invited to a big party in the Hamptons, we accepted without hesitation. I knew there would be

72

celebrities on hand, but that was not the big attraction. Nor was I excited about the prospect of a cocktail party—no, I hadn't sunk that low yet. The way I looked at it, it would be another one of those days when I didn't have to cook dinner.

The party was set in the home of Shana Alexander, the well-known author-editor-columnist, and the flavor of the party was decidedly literary. The gathering was intended to enable some of the people at *Newsday* to meet some of the writers who live on the Island.

Again in the company of Lou and Stella, we were among the first arrivals. It was a lovely home on a windswept dune leading down toward the ocean. The carpets were shaggy, the paintings were interesting, the books were all the right ones, and the guests were impressive.

One of the first to arrive was Craig Claiborne. I had interviewed approximately a thousand celebrities in my life, but in Claiborne's presence I was tongue-tied.

"It's a pleasure to finally meet you," I said to him. "I mean it, a real pleasure."

Craig Claiborne looked at me with a trace of suspicion. He is a slight figure of a man, especially for a lover of good food, and he seemed to shrink even more before this onslaught. Heaven knows how many women have besieged him at one party or another but this may have been a novel experience for him.

"I've got to tell you," I said, "you've been saving my life all this year."

"Izzat so?"

His response was delivered in weary, mechanical tones. It was the politeness of a man waiting for someone to come along and rescue him.

"I'm serious," I went on. "Just two nights ago, I made your creamed chicken tarragon and it was tremendous. The beautiful thing is how simple it was. You know . . ."

"Oh, izzat so?"

"But you want to know what my favorite recipe of them all is?"

"Surely."

"Sole Albert," I said. "I've had some seafood dishes that compare with it, but only in France, and only at those two-star and three-star restaurants . . ."

"Sole Albert?" he said. "I don't remember that one. Are you sure it was in my cookbook?"

"Sure it was," I said. "It was in that first book, the blue one. You know, I still use that book almost every night. The great thing about it is how simple the recipes are but still, you know, impressive."

"It's odd how many of those recipes I've forgotten," he said. "People always come up to me with recipes from that book and I don't have the foggiest idea what they're talking about most of the time. Sole Albert—hmmmm?"

"And there's another one I want to ask you about."

"Yes," he said, "and you're going to tell me that this one didn't work out at all."

"No, it was great."

"That's odd. People usually like to tell me about the recipe that doesn't work out. Often as not, that's the only one they can remember."

I wondered whether he had been reading my mind. In fact, I had been planning to temper all this praise by mentioning his shrimp curry. Never before had I so severely mistreated shrimp. The recipe itself had called for an enormous outlay of effort and money and had resulted in a dish that seemed more Mexican than Indian, a kind of fruitlike chili, if that can be imagined. But now I didn't say a word.

"I saw the pictures of your new kitchen in *House Beautiful*," Corinne said. "It looked beautiful."

"It hasn't worked out well at all," he said. "I wish I could start from scratch and . . ."

He turned to Corinne with obvious relief, evidently pleased to talk to someone other than myself. Other women gathered, surrounded him, and I was edged away. As the guests arrived and filled the home, I was able to reflect on the fact that at this, my first star-studded party in many months, I had managed to be improperly dressed, one of the three men in the house wearing neckties.

One advantage to being in a roomful of writers, you don't have to worry about holding up your end of the conversation. It is almost always enough to introduce yourself, stand back, and listen. Since I was involved in nothing worth talking about, I lis-

74

tened. I heard the full details surrounding twenty-seven different works-in-progress and at least that many book contracts, generally described as "fat."

A few people in the room knew who I was, and one of the publishers on hand, a slightly overpowering man named Norman, was positively flattering. In fact, he seemed so amiable that I decided to tell him what I was doing with myself.

"We've really been missing your column," he said. "The paper hasn't seemed the same, and a lot of us have been wondering what you're up to."

"Well, that's nice to hear."

"So what do I tell 'em? What *are* you up to these days?"

Did I dare? Why not?

"I'm doing the housework."

"What are you talking about, housework?"

"I mean I'm taking care of things at home this year. My wife is paying all the bills and I'm taking care of the house and the family."

"Ha-ha-ha!" Norman was one of those people who laugh the way it's written in comic books. "That's rich! Really, what've you been doing with yourself?"

"I'm being serious," I said. "Ask my wife—she's right over there. She's been going off to work every day and I've been taking care of the kids. I'm doing the cleaning and the cooking and . . ."

"Ha-ha-ha!" Louder this time. "C'mon, what're you up to? You're working on a novel but it's a secret, right?"

"No," I said. "Really. I am doing the housework."

"Someone like you, I can just imagine it," he said. "You're some kidder."

He went on along that line and I must say it was flustering. Norman was unaware of the fact that several women had edged closer to the conversation and were listening to him rather intently. They seemed to be reacting to him in a similar manner. The word I'm looking for is revulsion.

"Listen to this!" Norman didn't know when to stop. "Mike McGrady here says he's staying home and taking care of the kids and cooking and ha-ha-ha . . ."

"So what's so funny?" one of the women asked.

At this moment Norman realized that he had managed to insult at least half the human race and he started an awkward retreat toward the bar. The women then turned to me and I have seldom basked in such open approval. They were all stylish women, the kind of women who were wearing sunglasses propped up in their hair that year, giving the impression that they all possessed a second set of eyes. Another fashion innovation, they were all wearing men's shirts and leaving the top three or four buttons undone. This established beyond reasonable doubt that most of them had breasts and what made this even less a matter of conjecture was the fact that they had all decided to go without brassieres. This phenomenon led to another one, the sideways conversation—throughout the room, women were talking to empty space directly in front of them while their escorts of the moment stood over to the side, peering down.

When the women heard that I was working in the home while my wife was free to run her business, I found myself the center of attention. I'm sure my eyes gave away the fact that I was not yet a fully liberated human, but these sophisticated women did not seem to mind in the least. After a while, Corinne joined the gathering, held onto my arm, and introduced herself. There were at least trace elements of metal in her voice, and the next thing I knew, all those sophisticated women moved on.

"Hey, you chased all the broads away."

"I didn't mean to," Corinne said. "It's just that I had to escape from your friend Norman. He keeps telling me that I should let you go back to work. And he spits when he talks."

Aided in no small way by the lubricants, I walked through this mélange of writers and politicians and editors, telling one and all what it was like to be a housewife. At one point I managed to tell our hostess Shana Alexander that she was the loveliest woman I had even seen. Shana Alexander did not seem overly impressed by the compliment, not nearly so impressed as Corinne was.

"I think we should be going," she told me.

"What's the matter, honey? Have I had too much to drink?"

"It's not that," she said. "It's just that Shana Alexander just said the most awful thing."

"What was that?"

"Well, she was looking at Stella and myself and I heard her say,

'Oh, look at the *Newsday* wives—how pretty and young they are!' "

"What a terrible put-down!" I said. "I'm sure we can get her to apologize for saying something like that. I'll go over to her right now and demand a retraction."

"It *is* terrible," Corinne said. "I'm so tired of being a *Newsday* wife. I thought that was behind us now. For the first time in quite a few months I'm Mrs. Mike McGrady again and to tell you the truth, I'm hating it."

It was time to leave. On the way out I stopped for a moment to talk with Willie Morris, the novelist and former *Harper's* editor, who was standing in a far corner fending off admirers. I had met Willie a few times in the past, had once gotten thoroughly smashed in his company, and had long admired his work.

"What're you doing, Mike?"

I couldn't tell him what I was doing. I've got no excuse, but there was just no way to tell him the truth.

"Oh, you know," I said, "I'm kicking around a couple of book ideas."

No matter. It was still one hell of a party, one of many we went to during the course of our upside-down year. If you asked us to a party that year, we came. You could have been a crashing bore, a militant right-winger, a rifle collector, all of these, it didn't matter. If there was a free dinner involved, a night off, we were there with bells on.

ELEVEN

Last year, before doing this, I was appalled by what I perceived to be an abysmal lack of household organization. I became most keenly aware of this disorganization whenever I started to look for something. Whether I needed a hammer, a screw driver, a pair of socks, or a kitchen knife, I would carry the problem to the only person in the house who understood our elaborate and complicated filing system, the permanent manager of the McGrady family Lost & Found Dept. That, of course, was Corinne.

Sometimes—not often, you understand, but sometimes—she would not be able to locate the item at once. I would then give vent to my frustration with an expression that will be familiar to anyone in charge of running the family's Lost & Found Dept.: "Why can't I ever find anything around this place?"

One day, approximately two years before our switch, Corinne stopped. Just stopped. She stopped filing everything and she stopped finding anything. When anyone in the family began a sentence with "Where is . . ." she would flash one of her sweetest smiles and offer a response that never varied: "I don't know." This was not a sudden failing of memory on her part; it was a conscious decision to give up a relatively unrewarding career in the lost-and-found field. It was, I now realize, part of a large process, part of the education of four people who had come to prize their time more than Corinne's. The results were entirely predictable; we learned how to find things on our own. It was either that or do without. Sometimes we did without, but more often we conducted independent searches.

My first task, on assuming control of the household, would be one of organization. I knew it would be a challenge, but I was spurred on by a vision. I imagined the house as it might be, rather like a huge clock, each component running smoothly, meshing synchronously with all related components. My initial chore, then, would be one of designing—or redesigning—the basic systems and coming up with a smoothly functioning, self-lubricating machine.

I suffered no qualms about this, no secret failings of confidence. Nor did I take pains to keep my vision from Corinne. One day she would observe that the pantry was an unqualified mess and I would say, "Don't worry, I'll have all that straightened out as soon as I take over." On another occasion she would ask the whereabouts of a new potato peeler and I would say, "Don't worry, you'll be able to find all those things the minute I'm in control—I'll set aside a separate drawer for them." And should she be heard to complain about the towels heaped on the laundry-room floor, she would hear this: "I'm thinking about installing a new linen closet, then you won't see those towels."

My attitude was as thoroughly irritating to Corinne as it would be to anyone who had spent the previous two decades establishing her own set of systems. But it was not without its beneficial side effects. A week before I took over the housekeeping duties, I noticed a series of profound changes. Day after day I came home to find Corinne, sometimes with her friend Stella, bandana wrapped around her hair, painstakingly cleaning and reorganizing every shelf and drawer in the house.

Before a system can be changed, it must be understood. The first days had been spent trying to come to grips with the present organizational schemes. Not a thing was changed. In truth, I was content to simply hang on, to survive. By the end of the first week I had not even made a stab at a task absolutely basic to housewifery, the cleaning of the clothes.

Initially, I saw this as no major problem, certainly not one requiring any organizational genius. Just a month or two earlier, Corinne had moved the washer and the dryer up from the basement to the brand-new laundry room. The iron and ironing board were now located just a few convenient steps away from the washer and the dryer. No, I didn't see the cleaning of clothes as any momentous problem, and, in fact, I planned to do my first wash while setting out the Friday evening dinner, the old two-birds-with-one-stone dream.

Before starting dinner, I went through the bedrooms, collecting all the dirty clothes in sight and adding them to the clothes already piled high on the laundry-room floor. Then—ah, the marvels of our modern times—I twisted a couple of knobs, jabbed a couple of buttons. The fact that there were two sets of knobs and buttons—one for the washer, the other for the dryer—did not seem overly bothersome.

Indeed, by ten o'clock, during the hours set aside for the dinner and dishes, the week's laundry was processed. That is, it was washed and dried. Now it just had to be ironed and sorted. By two in the morning, with the rest of the family sound asleep, I was still at it.

And there, in the quiet hours, I made several new discoveries. I learned that the clothes worn by a fourteen-year-old boy are not all that different than the clothes worn by an 11-year-old boy or, for that matter, the clothes worn by a thirteen-year-old girl. I learned, further, that the two females in the family, Corinne and

Siobhan, have markedly similar tastes in garments ranging all the way from jeans to nightgowns.

There had been nothing in my background to prepare me for the sorting of the socks. I washed, as nearly as I could determine, three dozen pairs of socks, all of them wool, most of them in varying shades of gray. For the first five minutes, it was a game. For the next half hour, a challenge. Thereafter, a monumental pain. With about one third of the socks successfully remated, I gave up and turned my attention to the iron.

It seemed strange but I couldn't remember the last time I had seen Corinne standing in front of an ironing board. The only times I could recall her with an iron in her hand occurred about ten minutes before we were due to arrive at one party or another. Come to think of it, those were the only times I had seen her seated at a sewing machine.

Well, this was a new regime. At the outset I had planned to iron everything. Everything! I would be wearing uncreased shirts and sleeping on freshly pressed sheets; by God, I would even iron the towels. Naturally enough, I began by ironing my clothes. Yes, first things first. For many of my garments this was the first ironing and some didn't seem to know how to react properly—they hung onto their wrinkles with determination or they revealed an alarming tendency to turn brown at a touch of heat. It was more complicated than first it appeared. At two in the morning, some three hours beyond my normal hour of retirement, the kitchen was filled with small piles of clothing, miniature mountains decorating range top and cutting board and sink. At that hour I surrendered and unplugged the iron.

Granted, the laundry system was imperfect. Granted, too, the problem was not one that would be solved overnight. In fact, I did not even try to confront the issue immediately—the clothing remained scattered through several rooms of the house until individual family members came and retrieved their respective garments.

Before tackling the laundry a second time, I waited for one of those days when Corinne would be in Manhattan for business. Thirteen days had passed since the first effort and the piles of clothing this time seemed higher, more imposing, somehow even more soiled. But this time I was not going to rush things, not going to panic. This time I would go at it slowly, analyze the system, seek to discover why it is failing.

So much can be done when you understand the system. Understand the educational system and you'll get good grades. Understand the corporate setup and you'll rise within it. Why should laundry be any different?

By this time I was working out other systems as well, a system of systems. I had learned, for example, that it was impossibly taxing to cook a first-rate meal every night of the week. On those nights that Corinne was in the city late, I would revert to obsolete practices and take the kids out to a hamburger stand. Incidentally, that first trip back was a thoroughly chastening experience. Upon learning that the evening fare would be supplied by McDonald instead of McGrady: whoops of pure joy.

While the kids were wallowing in carbohydrates, I remained in the car and thought seriously about the dirty clothes, specifically about what I was going to do with all the dirty clothes cluttering up my closets and my life.

I could begin with this premise: whatever laundry system we had been using was a failure. In fact, even referring to it as a system gave it an unmerited glorification. And it was not that our methods lacked intricacy. The complicated process was inevitably triggered by one child's response upon learning that he had run out of some essential article of clothing—socks, say, or underwear. What happened at this juncture was that the child would go back and tunnel through his various piles of dirty clothing and find the garment that seemed least soiled, thus delaying the laundering process at least a day.

But eventually would come the reckoning, the moment when it could no longer be put off. The child in question would then take a stack of dirty clothes, put them in the washing machine, occasionally remember to add soap, and then take that essential final step and turn the machine on.

The clothes would be washed. Washed but not necessarily dried. A day or two later someone else would show up with another pile of soiled clothes and discover the earlier deposit lying wadded up in the bottom of the machine. Simple. The old load would be moved to the dryer, thus making room for the new load in the washer. And, at this time, should there be clothes in the dryer, they would be dumped on the floor, as often as not mixing in with dirty clothes that other members of the family had left there earlier.

This led to one of several possibilities. Either (a) the original owner of the clean clothes would come in and scream, "Who put my clean clothes on the floor?" Or (b) the clean clothes would intermingle with the dirty clothes and be washed a second time. Or (c) if the system was functioning at its peak, they might be washed a third and a fourth time before finally finding their way back to their rightful owner.

Nothing seemed clearer to me than the conclusion that the laundry should be done a single time. In all likelihood, then, it should be done in a single sitting—washed, dried, ironed, sorted, and distributed.

After dinner out, with the kids watching the Bob Hope show on television, I turned on the various laundering machines and set up the ironing board in the kitchen. I have known little in life more depressing than that experience, standing there ironing my daughter's massive wardrobe, listening to Bob Hope and actor Burt Reynolds trading tacky little jokes about the actor's affair with an older woman.

On second thought, it might have seemed as depressing without the television set on. Any job requiring the constant repetition of a simple act is going to seem dumb. No assembly-line worker in Detroit, no person tightening the same bolt on the same door of every sedan coming out of the factory, ever put in more dummy time than a normal housewife.

Yet here, as with most other domestic tasks, a wandering mind is a thing of danger. I knew that many fabrics were not intended to be ironed, and while this fact is clearly stated on the labels, I did not always remember to read the labels. Corinne is still looking for what was once a fragile white blouse with mother-of-pearl buttons.

But I *was* learning. Before too long I stopped ironing towels and tee-shirts. The next to go were the sheets. Still, time ran out on me—it was past midnight—and I was just getting around to the sock-sorting system. An hour later there remained twenty-three socks with no apparent mates. My temptation was to sweep the bachelor socks into the garbage can and be done with them, but common sense kept telling me that at some subsequent time I would have to dispose of twenty-three other lonely socks.

Shortly before two in the morning, I became aware of the fact that Corinne had not yet returned from her day in the city. What in the hell was going on? Her usual time of arrival was nine or ten at night. Just as I was imagining the worst—picturing her in the arms of a handsome young designer—she came breezing in, her face still alight with the pleasures of the long day, telling me about closing one business deal after another and then going to Lutèce Restaurant with Stella for a celebratory splurge.

Lutèce—the name was enough to make me misty-eyed, thinking back to the good old days of white tablecloths, gleaming silver, expense accounts. But back then, even when I was working, I had never hazarded Lutèce. I had been told that a person could spend a hundred dollars there without seriously violating a diet. I tried to imagine Corinne there in that fancy restaurant without me. How could she possibly manage? All too well, judging by the expression on her face.

Months went by without my solving the laundry problem. The only system that got any results at all—and those were, at best, temporary—required that I assemble the three children and yell at the top of my voice until all the clothes disappeared from sight.

Still, the day I dreaded most of all was Ironing Day. I found ways to delay that event as long as possible. By the time I got around to setting up the board, there would be several weeks' worth of laundry, a half-dozen basket loads, awaiting my service.

More items that I had once ironed were now simply folded, and I was making greater use of the children for such things as sock sorting. The distribution of other clothes was accomplished by putting everything in one pile, summoning the entire family, saying, "Take what's yours." There was something about the sight of all that clothing that seemed to cause a form of temporary amnesia. By the time they had, for example, culled out the socks, I still had enough left over to outfit a regiment of one-legged men.

During Ironing Day itself, I spent what seemed to be an inordinate amount of time working on Siobhan's clothes. Standing there, pressing the wrinkles from all those slightly frilly dresses, I would

83

occasionally feel a pleasant, old-fashioned, male-chauvinist glow. I could imagine how the dresses would look on her, how pretty she would be. This image vanished one day about halfway through the year. I had just ironed three pairs of Siobhan's slacks. They were her favorites and they were becoming increasingly familiar to me. I had ironed the same slacks the time before and, indeed, the time before that and . . .

"Siobhan," I said, "how long do you wear a pair of slacks?"

"Usually two days," she said.

"*Two* days?"

"Sometimes one day."

"*One* day?" Surely she was putting me on. "You know how long I'm going to wear these pants? At least a week, that's how long."

"That's why they look so yucky," she said.

My sense of timing did leave something to be desired. At that moment I happened to be wearing work clothes, a pair of antique corduroys that were streaked with grime and oil and white paint. They managed to cut the very heart out of my argument. I looked over at my thirteen-year-old daughter, as always calm and unruffled. She was, I noticed, wearing a frilly white blouse that I had ironed just moments earlier.

"Siobhan," I said, "how come you're wearing that nice blouse on a Saturday when you don't even have to go to school?"

"But it's my *favorite!*"

It was not, to my way of thinking, an adequate explanation. It simply reinforced my feeling of futility, the realization that our current laundering system was a disaster.

Liam, too, presented a problem, an opposite problem. I could never charge him with over-working the launderer. Weeks would pass by before I laundered a garment that seemed to belong to him. Liam would wear some favored items—for example, a sweat-shirt bearing the emblem of a local basketball team—until they could be removed in strips. One day I finally succeeded in separating him temporarily from his "Property-of-the-Knicks" sweater. I washed it and we were all surprised to learn that it was not red-and-gray; it turned out to be pure gray, and the red must have been a splattering of tomato soup.

One day late in the year I finally decided to resign as family launderer. I had just ironed a red plaid hunting shirt. Through the months, that shirt had become quite familiar to me. I had washed, dried and ironed this same shirt every laundry day. But whose shirt was it? I had bestowed much lavish care on this particular shirt and I had never seen anyone wearing it. Was it possible that it wasn't being worn? Was it even remotely possible that I had been doing all that work for a shirt no one was wearing?

"Whose shirt is this anyway?"

"I never saw it before," Siobhan said.

The thought was first chilling, then enraging. This shirt that no one had apparently worn was terribly difficult to iron. It was one of those slightly fuzzy wool shirts that tends to adhere to a hot iron; it had to be done at special low setting and even then with great caution.

"That used to be my shirt," Sean said. "But I outgrew it last year—no one wears it."

"Let me get this straight," I said. "You don't wear this shirt any more but somehow it manages to find its way into the washing machine every week."

"Don't blame me," he said. "I never touch it."

"Then how in the hell does it manage to get into the wash every week?"

"Don't ask me," he said.

"I don't know," Siobhan said.

"Well, you can both kiss this shirt good-by," I said. The shirt had become a symbol—a fuzzy, plaid, impossible-to-iron symbol of the apparently endless futility of this job. "It's the end of the road for this shirt."

I took the shirt from the ironing board and made a production out of ripping off the sleeves, first the right one, then the left. Then I balled up the entire thing and threw it into the fireplace. My destructive urges were not yet completely satisfied and so I crumpled up some newspapers and put them under the shirt and I got the matches and started a small bonfire. Watching that shirt go up in smoke was a gloriously satisfying moment; it burned every bit as beautifully as I knew it would.

"Hey!" Liam had come into the room and was watching the fire. "Who burned up my good shirt?"

It was then that I developed the laundry system that is in effect here today. The new system is based on the premise that it is absurd for any one person to clean another person's clothing.

"I've got some good news and some bad news," I told the family at dinner. "First, the good news. Starting next week, everyone gets a fifty-cent-a-week increase in allowance."

"Yeah, and what's the bad news?" Sean asked.

"And, starting next week, everyone does their own laundry. Washing, drying, ironing—everything. To make things easier, I have gotten each of you a brand-new laundry bag and a brand-new laundry basket. I never want to hear about your laundry problems again and I never want to see your dirty clothes again."

The three of them took the laundry bags and the baskets and their faces told the story. Liam, imagining what fifty cents a week might mean on the baseball-card market, was overjoyed. Sean, always the realist, was glum. And Siobhan was shattered—but then, it's never easy for a person to lose a valet.

TWELVE

"You know, there's still one thing you haven't tried to do," Corinne was saying. "You haven't yet had anyone come over for a formal dinner party."

"I'm not ready for that yet."

"Sure you are," she said. "Your cooking is good enough and there's no reason to be afraid. And the way you've been accepting dinner invitations, we're beginning to owe a lot of people return invitations."

"I've got to practice first. I couldn't just begin by making dinner for a dozen people."

"Why don't you start with your family then? If the dinner doesn't come out perfectly, they may even forgive you."

On a warm Sunday in spring I took the plunge and invited my

entire family—father, mother, brother and his family—out for dinner. I decided to limit the menu to foolproof dishes. I would begin with a *gazpacho,* the same recipe that Ernest Hemingway once used, and then I would serve mussels picked fresh from a nearby beach and steamed open in wine, butter, garlic, and parsley. The main dish presented something of a problem; I didn't want to try something too showy or too predictable. I settled finally on a New England pot roast cooked in a cranberry-horseradish sauce. And for dessert, a chocolate cake baked the morning of the party.

I plotted out the dinner in detail. The first and last courses would be prepared ahead of time. And then, while the pot roast was simmering, I would steam open the mussels, giving everyone the impression of being hard at work. Yes, the final fifteen minutes, I would be orchestrating a half-dozen pots and pans simultaneously. Oh, it was going to be a beautiful meal, a grand performance, a stunning dinner party until the very moment I fell off a balcony.

The family had arrived and the picture taking had commenced. I went up the ladder to my loft-study to get something and I came down by the most direct route. Either the cat finally succeeded in tripping me or the rolling ladder rolled or I simply managed to miss the top, and all subsequent, rungs of the ladder. No one saw the fall, but everyone heard it. As it turns out, a two-hundred-pound body falling ten feet onto a hardwood floor makes considerable noise on impact. Since one of the key points of impact was my head, most of the details are fuzzy. The fact that I did land on my head enabled me to sleep through the next half hour, despite six broken ribs, a broken collar bone, and a dented nose.

Only later did I discover how my family reacted to all this. My mother was doing just fine as long as she remained in the other room and didn't see me. She was doing just fine, that is, until an ambulance driver sought to reassure her.

"Don't worry, ma'am," he said, "it's just a lot of blood."

"Blood!" she said. "What blood?"

My father, a medical writer for many years, took one look at the gasping, wheezing, bleeding hulk of a son and did one of the bravest things imaginable—he attempted mouth-to-mouth resuscitation. I've been told that this caused me to revive momentarily, at least long enough to say, "Enough already!"

When I awakened, I was in a moving ambulance, looking up at the faces of the men who had carried me there. They seemed concerned. What they were most concerned about was what had happened to their backs when they carried me.

"How much do you weigh anyway?" one of them said.

"Oh, about two hundred and ten pounds."

"Jesus," he said. "We always get the heavy ones."

As we drove to the emergency room of the nearest hospital, I could hear the whispered speculations—phrases like "broken back" and "broken neck" came through quite clearly. Suddenly another concern hit me: had I left the heat on under the pot roast?

"What pot roast?" someone said.

I hadn't realized I was talking out loud. There was no way I could expand on that theme so I sought to change the subject.

"Are we going to Huntington Hospital?"

"No," I was told. "This is an emergency, so we're going directly to the country club."

What started within me as a nice hearty laugh ended quickly in a gasp. It only hurt when I laughed. And also when I sneezed, coughed, sighed or just hazarded a deep breath.

Emergency room. X-ray room. Surgical theater to sew up the nose. Finally, after being poked by a dozen different doctors, a room, a room with a wall clock. It was just the time I should have been serving the pot roast. I was wondering whether Corinne would be able to take over and handle everything. The possibility that the family was not going ahead with dinner as planned had not yet occurred to me. Later I learned that they, too, were waiting to hear whether my spine had been broken.

Who, I was wondering, would get the kids off to school in the morning? Corinne didn't know what food was on hand and what supplies were needed. I imagined it would be chaotic for her until I could get back home and take over. At the same time, I sensed that it was a good thing this had happened to me and not to Corinne; without her income, we would have been in some trouble. Fortunately, I was the housewife and that was the difference between inconvenience and disaster—the family had lost its servant, not its income.

Well, inconvenience for the rest of the family, disaster for me. That first night I began to feel the results of the tumble. My bed was elevated to a thirty-degree angle and I was strapped to the mattress, unable to slide an inch in either direction.

Corinne came into the room late that night and she experienced some difficulty in looking at me. Three days later, when I was finally able to study myself in a mirror, I could understand why. My face was a mass of bruises, a rainbow of discolorations. When a nurse looks away from you in horror, you can be sure you've lost some of your natural beauty.

"You did this on purpose, didn't you?" Corinne said. "You just didn't want to have to make that dinner for everyone."

"My *dinner*—what happened to it?"

"We just had the soup and the mussels," she said. "That's all anyone felt like. We'll have enough pot roast left over for the rest of the week."

"But did they like it?" I asked.

"No one said a word."

Well, all in all, my first dinner party had not been a complete success. Of course, when most of the guests feel that the host is a goner, it can tend to take the edge off the appetite. Corinne had taken one look at me lying in a puddle of my own blood and had been convinced that I was dead. I must say, this had its good side. During the weeks and months that followed, she treated me with the kind of affection I hadn't known before.

Before too long, in fact, I found a full set of silver linings to go with this accident. Even a kind of relief that for a while I could sleep late and forget about getting three kids off to school. Relief that I no longer had to pretend to clean the house. In addition, there was something quite nice about being waited on again.

The following day, as the pain was coming into full blossom, I was just settling down to the not entirely unpleasant prospect of telling everyone about my accident. There seemed no more logical place to begin than with the man sharing my hospital room.

Unfortunately, he beat me to the punch. He began by saying that he had two weeks to live, possibly three. While he was waiting to be lifted from the stretcher to the bed beside my own, he explained that the cancer had gone through his blood and was now in his bone marrow. He said that his weight had dropped from 200 pounds to 145. Then he told me not to waste time worrying about him—after all this pain, the thought of death didn't seem half bad.

"But how're *you* feeling?" he asked.

"Terrific," I said. "Just fine."

In fact, I was hurting like hell. The broken ribs, the broken collar bone, the cut face—but none of this seemed worth dwelling on at the moment. And during the next three days, while my roommate was leapfrogging toward the pearly gates, I was unable to do so much as shift my weight around. But there is simply no way to complain effectively when your only audience is dying of cancer, so I spent those three days trying to keep my groans to myself.

My first genuine opportunity to complain came when they rolled me down for my final visit to the X-ray room. I was deposited at the end of a long line of stretcher-borne patients. The man on the next stretcher was covered by a sheet but I could see the tip of a cast on his protruding right leg.

"How're you feeling?" I began.

"Not bad at all," he said.

"I see that you've broken your leg."

"Oh, they tell me I broke almost everything," he said. As he was talking, a nurse came over and removed the sheet. I noticed then that his leg cast did not stop at the thigh; it was simply one section of a body cast that extended from his feet to his throat. It had apertures to provide for the elimination of wastes. "And how're *you* feeling?"

"Can't complain," I said.

By God, wasn't that the truth! The half-dozen days in the hospital were at least restful. Until then, until I was forced to stop all motion, I hadn't realized how much actual running around I had been doing as a housewife. And until I had to eat hospital food, I hadn't realized how much progress I'd made as a cook.

The injuries did not suddenly disappear as I staggered out the hospital door. During the next month I slept in a rented electric bed and during the next ten days, Corinne was forced to care for me. What this meant, in effect, was that she would once again have to resume some of her old chores.

To observe that she was not too keen about this is to indulge in understatement. Now, I was in no position to be critical but I could not help but notice sudden departures from the practices I had followed over the most recent months. Instead of rising with the sun to make the kids breakfast and lunch, she slept to the usual hour and allowed them to shift for themselves. Instead of carrying lunch with them, they bought lunch in the school cafeteria.

However, as I say, I tried not to criticize. Besides I was enjoying the feeling once again of having someone wait on me. It brought back memories of my old life as a man. And there was an added plus. I would lie there groaning and whining and shuddering, popping pain pills like an addict, and I must say I found it a great pleasure at last to be in a place where no one had a more serious ailment than myself.

It was also an opportunity to take stock physically. Doctors checking my blood pressure discovered that it had dropped twenty points in the four months since I left my job. My weight had dropped twenty pounds. And this was just a hint of things to come. By the end of a full year as a housewife, my blood pressure was as close to normal as it had ever been, and I had not felt that well physically in many years.

Then, rather abruptly, I stopped feeling so well. The doctor bills arrived.

Let me note at the outset that there is not an awful lot that modern medicine can do for broken ribs and clavicle. I managed to go through the entire experience without a doctor applying a piece of tape or making a single incision. What the doctors—four of them—did was look at the X-rays and make sure that my back wasn't broken. The other thing they did for me was make out a prescription for pain pills.

This is not to imply that the doctors were idle. One thing they seemed to do quite a lot of is make out bills. The Blue Cross insurance policy picked up the hospital tab of a thousand dollars but Corinne had to pay for the individual doctors bills. But how much could that possibly be? It turned out that the orthopedic surgeon, a charming young man who made a morning habit of sticking his head into the room and saying, "How're we feeling today?" before moving on, charged twenty-five dollars for each and every greeting.

And his was not the bill that proved most disturbing. The bill that bothered me most came from a doctor who had materialized in the emergency room at the time of my arrival. Speaking to me through my haze of pain, he had asked me if he should sew up my nose.

"Oh, does it require stitches?" I had asked.

"Oh yes," he had assured me.

We were together a grand total of two minutes, maybe three. He had gotten out needle and thread and he had sewn in a grand total of three stitches, maybe four, on a tiny cut on the bridge of my nose. Ten days later when I went to his office to have the thread removed, his receptionist handed me a bill for $125. She may have noticed my sudden pallor because she offered a quick explanation: "That covers the consultation, the surgery and the after-care—do you have the money with you?" There had been no consultation, no surgery, and there was not going to be any after-care.

Later, as Corinne was mailing him a check, I added a letter explaining why I wasn't writing the check: "The bill, in point of fact, hurt a great deal more than the nose injury itself. And it has left me slightly dazed. I find that every time I start to write a check out to that figure, my hand starts to tremble with rage." I then canceled all possible after-care: "I find my meetings with you have been much too costly."

I got a letter back from the doctor who admitted that other patients had also complained about his fee but usually changed their minds later: "These patients realized that I was called in consultation and came to treat them at any time of day or night, weekday or weekend without slightest hesitancy, no matter how large or small an injury had been sustained." He had a suggestion for anyone who questioned his fee: "I have welcomed their inquiry with the County Medical Society."

It seemed like an excellent suggestion and I followed it. Then I could understand why he would welcome such an inquiry; the County Medical Society wrote to inform me that he was not a member and that they could, therefore, take no action.

"I don't know why you're taking this so seriously," Corinne told me. "I really don't mind paying any of these bills."

"No one does," I said. "That's the trouble. That's why these guys can make such a fortune."

"I'm just happy to have you back alive."

I knew if positions were reversed, I would be saying exactly the same things she was saying now. But the medical bills were becoming a monumental issue in my mind. Why was that? I was at least as relieved as Corinne to be back home alive and well. But this time the bills aroused some feeling of guilt in me. The fact that I was not paying them made the fall from that ladder seem just that much dumber.

Another thing, money was changing in my mind, was looming larger than it ever had. The year before I could have dropped five hundred dollars at a poker game without a second thought. And now I was frenzied at the thought of the same amount of money going to a far worthier cause.

What had happened was simple; I had stopped getting a pay check. The hundred-dollar-a-week allowance was not enough to cover food and incidentals. I had dipped into the savings account at a fifty-dollar-a-week rate, and I was becoming aware of the rapidity with which money can disappear.

THIRTEEN

One responsibility often assumed by the woman of the house is the teaching of basic etiquette to the children. I had never gotten too deeply involved in this aspect of their upbringing before. But from time to time during the year I did try to point out the obvious *faux-pas*.

One day in mid-June, Tenny Davitian, one of Corinne's closest friends, came out from the city for a visit. As always, she brought her tiny dog, Daisy. I was pleased when both Sean and Siobhan greeted our city visitor promptly and politely. Liam, however, dashed through the room, ignored the guest, made a bee-line for the television set and switched on the cartoons.

"Liam!" I said. "Didn't you forget something?"

"What?"

93

"Didn't you forget to say hello to someone?"

He got up from the chair, walked back into the kitchen, looked at all of us and finally spoke up.

"Oh, I didn't see you." He was talking to the dog. "Hiya, Daisy!"

FOURTEEN

"Did you have a hard day at the office, dear?" I would ask.

"Don't ask," she would say.

This small exchange, with natural variations, took place more and more frequently as the year went on. Being a business person was taking a toll and it could be measured in visible ways. Corinne's appearance seemed increasingly run down, her face seemed paler, and there was a tightness that reflected the new tensions she was feeling.

I could easily remember the pleasure she once got from turning a hundred-dollar profit over the course of a week. This year there were some days when she would cash checks totaling a thousand dollars and more, but there was nothing to it, no pleasure. It had stopped becoming money; now it was part of a flow that exited her life as fast as it entered it.

"Oh, what a day!" she would say. "You're not going to believe what happened today!" she would say. "Those bastards!" she would say.

I would not ask her to elaborate until later, until she had gotten a hot dinner into her. And then there was no need to request the details. They would come out in a rush—a continuing chronicle of unreliable warehousemen, striking truckmen, unscrupulous competitors, overpriced raw materials, and foul-ups everywhere. During past years Corinne had been able to take such matters in stride, but then it had been something of a game. Then the profits had gone for extras, for luxuries, and now they kept a roof overhead and food in the refrigerator. Now it mattered.

The year chosen for the experiment happened to be a time of national economic uncertainty—a fuel shortage followed by a recession followed by unemployment followed by more inflations. People who had always paid accounts promptly began delaying; those who had delayed just stopped.

That year businessmen everywhere were discovering a new tool, something called a "chapter eleven." The phrase referred to a law designed to keep marginal businesses alive. It was not unlike a declaration of bankruptcy with this one distinct advantage: after paying a percentage of debts to creditors, the businessman was allowed to stay in business. Well, the year was a golden age for chapter elevens, also a golden age for not getting paid. The one sure way you could tell that a company was getting ready for a chapter eleven, the company would start placing unusually large orders.

To try and get a large percentage of the money owed her, Corinne often used the services of a prominent collection agency. One day in September we found out just how bad things had gotten.

"What happened today, dear?"

"This."

She handed me a check from the collection agency. It was a check made out for six hundred dollars and change and it had been bounced back by the bank, stamped "Insufficient Funds."

One of the motivating factors behind the experiment had been to permit Corinne to spend more time on her business than ever before. I must say she took advantage of it, working longer and longer hours as the year wore on. And although her business prospered, the pressure on her was mounting at a similar rate.

Just as Corinne had been looking forward to a full year in an office, so I had been looking forward to a full year of golf. I imagined an army of wage slaves trundling off to work every morning while I marched in an opposite direction, out toward the links. However, observing the effort Corinne was making at work introduced an element I hadn't anticipated—guilt. Before trying a single game of golf, I allowed the entire summer to pass me by. It was not until September that I finally found an excuse to play golf. I parred the last four holes, shot a 43 on the back nine, and was a goner for the rest of the year.

Day after day, I went out onto courses deserted by men who had put aside the games of summer for the pursuit of the buck. I played in frost and in light drizzles and in lengthening shadows and I would get home at dusk and throw something on the skillet just before Corinne arrived from another long day of commerce.

"You'll never believe what happened today," she said.

"What was that?"

"You'll never believe it."

"Try me."

"Oh, I don't want to depress you."

There I was, tanned and well-rested, free of all tension and responsibility, thinking of nothing more challenging than the 441-yard par-four fourteenth hole. What Corinne was thinking about was her newest product—a free-standing Lucite salad stand. The large, clear salad bowl was supported by three legs joined together by an ingenious three-way bolt. The product had required an initial commitment of twelve thousand dollars, and Corinne was observing its progress with a measure of anxiety. The major breakthrough came when the new salad stand was ordered in volume by Bloomingdale's, New York's trend-setting department store.

"You won't depress me," I said. "Tell me what went wrong."

"Don't ask."

"Okay, forget it."

"I'll tell you what went wrong," she said. "The salad stand isn't working. It's the damn three-way bolt. It's not holding the tripod together. People are sending them all back to Bloomingdale's. I don't know what to do."

There was nothing for me to say. Any business advice I might give Corinne would be ignored and should be ignored. And possibly because of a lack of practice through the years, I was not too successful at offering encouragement and reassurance. My inability to alleviate the situation in no way impaired my ability to suffer along with Corinne. I had learned a sad truth: the home keeper never experiences the mate's triumphs as richly as the failures. When Corinne had a triumphant day—a frequent occurrence, judging by the way she was supporting her family—my reward, often as not, was a simple absence of tension. But when the day was a wipe-out, there was no way for her to conceal that fact from me.

"If I lose Bloomingdale's, that would be real trouble."

96

"Oh, you won't lose . . ."

"I might," she was saying. "There's a new buyer over there. And you don't know how a store hates to have anything returned."

"Well, let's talk about it over dinner."

"I'm not hungry."

What I was thinking was, It's too bad she doesn't drink. I was beginning to understand why so many businessmen headed for the bar car or an at-home martini before subjecting their families to their adventures.

Over the next few days Corinne functioned in a panic, and the problems got solved. That night she was on the phone with the manufacturer. The next morning she was redesigning the stand's support system and lengthening the three-way bolt. Within the week she was visiting every branch of Bloomingdale's and replacing each set of defective legs with the new model.

Even as that problem was being solved, new ones appeared. In the busy season before Christmas, the United Parcel deliverymen voted to go on strike. Some businesses halted all deliveries for the duration of the strike; others hired their own trucks and some went out of business. Corinne took to awakening at dawn, driving to her warehouse and carting packages herself to the post office where she would sometimes stand on line for the better part of an hour.

A single problem like a United Parcel Service strike would set off a string of new problems. The post office, as it turned out, was a good deal harder on packages. This, in turn, led to increased breakage, more returns, short sharp notes from old customers. It led, finally, to the careful repacking of all products, to fewer hours in the day, to decreased profits, to a wife who inevitably came home worn down by the problems of business.

The pressures were felt by all of us. It was a Tuesday night in October, and, as usual, Corinne was working late. I was trying to decide whether to feed the kids or make them wait. And while I was in the process of deciding this, the food was losing its moisture, its freshness, its color. It was a good thing I am not a suspicious sort; Corinne had been late so often lately that she could have been conducting three or four affairs simultaneously. Finally,

I called the kids to the dinner table, and, as they were sitting down, we heard the sound of the car driving up to the house.

"I wonder what she's going to say tonight," Siobhan said.

"She's going to say, 'I'm sorry I'm late,'" Sean guessed. "That's what she always says."

"No," Siobhan said, "it's not late enough for that one yet. She's going to see us sitting at the table and she's going to say, 'Oh, what time is it?'"

"You're both wrong," I said. "She's going to come in and she's going to say, 'Oh, am I late?'"

The sound of a car door. The sound of footsteps up the walk. The front door slamming. The quick footsteps as she came from the hallway into the kitchen.

"Oh, am I late?" she said, and seemed slightly surprised when her question was greeted by applause and laughter.

One reason Corinne was late was Vinnie. The United Parcel strike had led to her doing business with many new people. One of her temporary new associates was a truck-owner named Vinnie. Vinnie was six-foot-three and constructed exclusively of muscle—muscle that seemed to extend from his feet all the way to his scalp.

Because of the strike, Corinne was forced to see Vinnie frequently. At least twice a week Vinnie pulled his truck up to the office and loaded the cartons aboard. Vinnie seemed to have enormous difficulty getting packages to the proper destination, but his prices were reasonable and, most importantly, he was not on strike. Since it was a temporary situation, Corinne put up with Vinnie's evident intellectual shortcomings for his one evident virtue: availability.

During October, the most trying month in the history of Corinne's business, Corinne stayed late night after night while Vinnie loaded the cartons onto his truck. One night she was explaining to him that the larger cartons contained the larger items on her line and that furthermore, it was impossible for one of the small cartons to contain an object larger than itself. Suddenly she was aware that Vinnie was edging closer to her and simultaneously of the fact that they were the last two people left in the building.

"Hey," Vinnie said, "would you wanna give your truckman a little kiss?"

"Whaaaaaat?"

"Wanna give your truckman a little kiss?"

"Vinnie, my husband wouldn't like that one little bit." How quickly even the most liberated woman resorts to ancient tactics. "And he's a very big man. Much bigger than you are."

"Ah, I just meant on the cheek," he said.

"Vinnie, let's cut the nonsense and get these boxes moved."

The conversation ended there but not in Corinne's mind. When she came home that night she was furious.

"It makes me so damn mad when men behave like that."

"What do you want?" I asked. "Do you want me to go beat up Vinnie?"

"Of course not."

"Well, it's a good thing."

"What makes me angriest is the way I reacted," she said. "I still don't know what I should have told him."

"Tell him that you're going to tell his wife," I suggested. "That always slows me down."

"Not funny."

The next few days were not easy ones for Corinne. Her upset over the incident seemed to grow—not so much because of the proposition but because of her reaction to it. My feeling was that Vinnie did not even realize he had said anything out of line, that in his world a woman would accept the invitation as a frank compliment. And, in fact, the next time Vinnie saw Corinne, he repeated the compliment.

"Oh," he said, "I'll bet you've decided to give your truckman a little kiss."

This time, however, Corinne was ready for him.

"Vinnie, you are sadly mistaken. You may think you're being flattering but it is the most insulting thing I can imagine. I've been doing a lot of business with you. And if you expect me to go on paying good money for your services, you better stop treating me like someone you picked up on a street corner. Is that clear?"

"Yes," he said.

"And besides, if you try anything funny, I'm going to tell your wife."

FIFTEEN

For months I saved up all clothes with rips and tears, and finally, midway through August, I was ready to do the sewing. The machine is a fancy one, equipped with attachments that would enable me to sew buttonholes or elaborate designs, if that was my intention.

Corinne began by showing me how to thread the needle; it is easier to get into heaven than to thread a sewing-machine needle. The sewing itself, however, was a breeze. Nothing to it. In fact, by the time I had repaired several of the children's shirts, my creative nature began to take hold. Since I could handle a straight stitch so well, why not try one with a little flair? Perhaps one of those lightning-shaped stitches. And if that was so simple, why not try one even more elaborate, a cross-over? In no time at all, I was trying all the machine's switches. The sewing itself continued to come out beautifully until Corinne stopped in to check my progress. She turned over a pair of slacks and on the opposite side we could both see a mountain of coiled thread, a mass of thread that resembled Harpo's hair. I could tell from Corinne's first reaction—"Stop!" she shrieked—that this was not the way it was supposed to be.

"Admit it," Corinne said, "this time you *tried* to louse it up."

I admitted no such thing. And I will maintain to this day that no one could plan such an elaborately godawful stitch as the one I came up with.

SIXTEEN

July 1. The midway point. Siobhan had an early-morning appointment with the orthodontist. The major difference between this day and the first day of the experiment was approximately sixty degrees. There was a second difference as well. No longer did I waste my time sitting in a dentist's waiting room, surrounded by women's magazines. No, I sat outside the office in a parked car, listening to the radio and watching a steady procession of women leading their daughters to the tooth-straightener. Ah, how far I had come in just six months!

Siobhan came out, smiling a shiny smile, relieved that the ordeal was behind her for another month. Then, as we were driving toward home, I realized that the day was an anniversary, that it marked the middle of the year set aside for role reversal. From this point on, it would be downhill. How would I celebrate the anniversary? Well, there would be a food-shopping trip. A second dental appointment later in the day, this one for the boys. The arrival, late in the day, of my mother-in-law and father-in-law, and, of course, a special dinner of welcome for them.

I took the moment to reflect on my old life as a working male. It did not, at the moment, seem nearly so dreary as it had when I was in the process of living it. I had thought of my job as repetitive. God, I hadn't known what repetitive was.

The reflection continued. The midway point. What had I learned? What had I really done with all my new freedom? I had embarked on no major new reading program. I had not written a word in my spare time. I had undertaken no new projects. Instead, I had lost myself in the minutiae of my new life, had concentrated more and more on the fine details of organizing the existence of a family. Somewhere in the process I had lost track of myself and my life and my plans for a more meaningful existence.

And this day would be typical. Another day devoted to making life easier for others. A two-dentist day. A supermarket-shopping day. A company-dinner day. Just another ho-hummer in a long succession of ho-hummers. I was looking forward to the arrival of Corinne's parents not just because we've always liked each other but because their arrival would break up some of the routines.

I dropped off Siobhan and set off for the supermarket. I never reached my destination. I drove up to the supermarket, couldn't see an available parking space, and continued driving. When I stopped finally I was on the South Shore of Long Island at a topless bar known as the Body Shop. I had been there before, but as a columnist, for business reasons only. There was on any given afternoon a fine collection of barmaids, half-naked dancers, truck drivers, and brain surgeons, and if I could not get a column from such a collection of people, then I was not half trying. This time there was no business justification for my visit. There was no justification at all, and I don't think I'll bother trying to explain it.

Kathy, the barmaid, still handled the daytime shift. Kathy is a woman with an earthy laugh, an untroubled disposition, and a keen appreciation of the value of print.

"Hi, Kathy," I said.

"Hi . . . there," she said.

She turned her back on me and went for the Jack Daniel's bottle. She remembered the drink but not the name. As she brought the glass back to me, she asked how things were going, listened intently as I said okay, then studied my face, trying to place it. I turned around to see the latest word in mammaries.

"Hey." She couldn't stand it any longer. "What's your name anyway?"

"Mike," I said.

"Yeah, hey, Mike what?"

"Mike McGrady."

"Yeah," she said. "Didn't you used to come in here or something?"

"Yeah," I said. "I used to work on the newspaper."

"Oh yeah, that's right."

Kathy carried the report to the back room, to the owner of the Body Shop, and he came out with a handshake.

"You left the newspaper?" he asked.

"Yeah."

"That's why I don't see your picture there any more."

"I'm doing a book."

"What kind of book?" he asked.

"It's an illustrated history of topless bars in America," I said.

"Hey, that's a terrific idea," he said. "And you're not going to forget the Body Shop, am I right? Kathy, set up Mike here on the house. Enjoy the show, Mike."

The drinks were on the cuff. I was just starting to feel relaxed, when a rotund bearded man came up.

"Did I hear them say you were Mike McGrady?"

"That's right."

"Oh, this is terrific," he said. "I've been wondering what happened to you. Hey, Kathy, this next one is on me."

The fellow was creating such a stir that the other patrons looked away from the dancer and examined the visiting celebrity. Should a genuine celebrity ever wander into one of these places, he might take understandable pains to shield his identity. But it had been so long since my name had meant anything to anybody that I just relaxed and enjoyed it.

"You've got to do me this one thing," the bearded man was saying. "You've got to sign this piece of paper for me. Here, you've got to write down a little message. 'To my old pal and drinking buddy, Danny.' "

"What's this?" I said. "You trying to tell the writer what to write?"

"Ah no," he said. "You write anything you like. But it would just be nice if you got in that 'drinking buddy' someplace, you know, anyplace at all."

Danny, it developed, was a lover of literature. He remembered several of my old columns with a clarity that was astounding. He also had a poem folded in his wallet, a poem he wanted me to read. It was a poem from *So . . . Help Me Lord* by Alton Wilson, and it was a tribute to a wife. I read a few of the lines.

> *It awes me to know*
> *She gave her life to me.*
> *She follows me, soothes my nerves,*
> *Cooks my meals, irons my clothes,*
> *Loves me when I'm good,*
> *And . . . I think . . . when I'm bad.*

There was more to it than that, but I had read enough.

"Hey, that's terrific," I said. "I used to have a wife just like that."

"What happened?" Danny asked. "You split?"

"No, she just disappeared. She disappeared six months ago today."

"That's terrible."

"Oh, it's all right," I said. "She still lives with me."

Danny didn't understand a word of this but that fact didn't stop

103

a friendship from forming. Danny was an asphalt-siding magnate, and his busy season came in autumn. During the slow summer months, he went off to work every morning and by noon had checked into the Body Shop. One of the advantages to steady patronage was that all the dancers knew Danny by name and joined him between sets.

The first dancer, Maria, was a graduate of convent school, and when she joined us and began unreeling her life story, I could only wish I was still writing a column. Before too long, we were seated at the table with two off-duty topless dancers and Danny was passing around a picture of his wife and I was searching my wallet for one of Corinne. *Corinne! And* the dentist appointment. *And* the food shopping. *And* her parents.

I asked for the time and discovered that it was seven o'clock in the evening. It was one of the year's great failures. There had been other evenings, one or two of them, when I didn't get home in time to make dinner, but to fall down on so many responsibilities simultaneously, that was unique. I searched for change, found some, searched for a phone, found one, searched for some courage and came up empty. What would I tell Corinne? As I heard her voice, I was suddenly aware of the jukebox in the background and I wished I had found a quieter phone.

"Hello," she said.

"Hi," I said.

"Oh, hello, Mike."

For some reason, she sounded extremely cheerful. I had to wonder about the connection.

"Corinne, can you hear me?"

"Where are you?" she asked. "I've been worried about you."

"There's nothing to worry about," I said. "I'm at this topless joint on Sunrise Highway and I've had too much to drink and I don't think I should come home now."

"That's perfectly all right," she said.

"It is?"

"Oh sure," she said. "You just go ahead and do whatever you have to do and don't worry about a thing here. When you didn't show up, I took the boys to the dentist."

"Sorry about that."

"Yes," she said. "My folks are here now, but I don't want you

104

to worry about trying to get home. They've already called some friends and they're planning to go out and have dinner in a restaurant. We'll make do here. You just do what you have to do."

"And you're not mad at me?"

"Not in the least," she said. "You just drive carefully, darling, and we'll see you when we see you."

I had some trouble believing my ears. Corinne had always seemed reasonable to me, but this surely went beyond reasonableness. I put the telephone back on the hook and went back to the table. How could it be? How could a guy be lucky enough to find a woman willing to overlook something like this? She probably realized that it was the midway point and that in the first half year of the experiment there had not been another incident of this nature. Not one. Or maybe she was being so sweet and understanding because she had gotten home late from work so often herself. Maybe she realized that everyone needs an occasional blowout to relieve the tension. There had to be a logical explanation, some logical explanation, but I came away from the phone shaking my head. My new friend Danny was all sympathy.

"Hey, I'll bet the old lady really laid you out," he said. "I coulda told you—never call home this time of night. It gets this late, you might as well wait until ten or eleven. They're not going to get any madder."

"Wives don't understand husbands," the convent-schooled dancer said. "I never heard of a wife letting her husband have a little fun."

"You're not going to believe this," I said. "But she wasn't even mad. In fact, she told me not to come home until I get sober."

I was correct; at first, no one else at the table believed a word of it. But when I stayed there and switched to hot coffee, they started to believe. The two dancers agreed with me that I had a unique wife. Danny listened to the talk for a while, then got up and called his wife. When he came back to the table, his face was bright red.

"Was she mad?"

"Oh no," he said. "She's a good woman."

"That's great."

"But I think I better go home," he said. "It was nice meeting you."

Later, sober, driving home, I congratulated myself repeatedly on my selection of a mate. I began telling myself that the first six months hadn't been that bad after all. If something like this had happened in the old days, Corinne would have been upset. But now she was getting out into the world, getting around, seeing how things are done. The experience was clearly making her worldly, more tolerant.

In many ways it was a much better arrangement. Sure, I had to do some dumb things. But I never had it so easy, financially speaking. Corinne's business was picking up and she was happier than ever and she seemed to be enjoying life much more. The jobs I had to do—well, maybe they weren't the most glamorous jobs in the world—but I should count my blessings. A good family, a strong marriage, a wife that put other wives to shame with her understanding.

I was thinking: well, now it is halfway through the year and you are not doing half bad. You have become a good cook and can even handle a company dinner, provided you get home for it. And the kids, you've never been closer to the kids. For the first time in your life, you've had a chance to watch them grow. Terrific kids. And it works both ways. Just as you've gotten closer to them, so they've gotten closer to you.

And I was thinking: where does it hurt you anyway? True, you're not doing anything really creative and no one knows who you are any more—but what does that really mean? This has been a change in your life, a monumental change, and no one goes through a change of this scope without some sacrifices.

And I was thinking: and the marriage has never seemed stronger, never been able to withstand outside threats with greater ease. Corinne has never been more loving and neither have you. It has been a chance for both of you to grow. She has been able to concentrate on her business and now there is a sense of fulfillment to her, a kind of inner well being you never saw before. People seem to gravitate toward her these days. And just look at the way she reacted to the telephone call this evening. Totally unthreatened. Was there another wife in the country like that?

And, finally, I was thinking: yes, it has been difficult, but it has all been worthwhile.

By the time I reached home, it was past midnight and Corinne was in bed. Seldom have I walked into my house more filled with a sense of comfort and well-being. Her parents had not yet returned from their hastily arranged dinner out. Just as well. They were as understanding as Corinne—but there is something about the sight of a son-in-law coming home at midnight that is not terribly reassuring.

I made my way to the bedroom and gave Corinne a nice big hug. What was it like? It was like, if you can imagine it, trying to embrace a huge piece of ice.

"What's the matter?" I said.

"Don't you touch me," she said.

"What?"

"Just keep your hands to yourself."

I began to wonder whether I had walked into the right home. This could not be the same sweet-voiced and forgiving wife I had spoken to just a few hours earlier.

"What's wrong? Did something happen?"

"Oh, you don't love me," she said. "There's no one in this whole world who thinks about anything except their own goddamned skins."

"But . . ."

"I'm just grateful that my parents didn't come home before you. I'm happy they don't know what time you got in or in what condition. What would they have thought?"

"I'm a little confused," I said. "On the phone you were telling me to take my time getting home."

"When I was talking to you on the phone," she said, "they were standing right there beside me. You can understand—maybe you can understand—that I didn't want them to know your true condition. I didn't want them to think I would marry a man who would forget a child's dentist appointment, and forget that he was cooking dinner, and forget that his family was visiting him, and forget that we were all sitting around the phone waiting for a call from him. And then he calls and it is an hour past dinnertime and he is in a topless bar. I didn't think it would be wise to let them know all of that."

"But you said . . ."

"Let's drop it, shall we?" Corinne said. "I'll talk to you tomorrow when, hopefully, we'll both be better able to make sense."

She rolled away then.

107

I was thinking: here you are at the halfway mark and you are a flop as a housewife, a failure as a female. You don't like your life at all, not a bit of it, and you have not even picked up a vacuum cleaner in weeks. You are a bad launderer, a mediocre cook, and you are seeing too much of your children. Six months and you are desperate to be out making a living. You are halfway through an out-and-out disaster, surrounded by stupidities and suffering from a clear-cut case of penis envy.

SEVENTEEN

In September we were going to be paid our annual visit by a friend from Corinne's distant past, a former prep-school classmate, Claudia. Every autumn Claudia showed up and gave us a peek at a world we had only read about.

Early in life, Claudia had listened to a different drummer. When others her age were drinking themselves senseless, she was smoking a strange weed known as marijuana. When all about her were becoming engaged and married, she took lovers. She had never married, never had children, never sought gainful employment, never worried about the ways of the straight world and now, at age thirty-six, she might have been seen as an aging hippie by some. I had always looked upon her as a person chronically ahead of her times.

One reason we have always enjoyed Claudia's visits is that she has shown us the road not taken. If things had worked out a little differently for either of us, we, too, might have wound up moving restlessly from one commune to another, might have spent a decade in New Mexico composing poetic tributes to the mighty peyote, might have found time to master several Indian dialects, might have followed the Taoist religion, might have attached ourselves to every counterculture trend as it materialized. We never realized just how straight we were until Claudia paid us her annual visit.

"You're not going to like her," Corinne warned me this year.

"Not going to what?"

"You're not going to like Claudia this time," she said.

"I've always like Claudia," I said. "I *do* like Claudia. She's one of the few people from our past I thoroughly enjoy. Let's face it, Claudia's one of the few people we know who never sold out."

"I'm just warning you. This time you're not going to like Claudia."

I had no idea what she was talking about. If anyone would appreciate our current situation, our reversal of roles, it would be Claudia. Maybe this time we would not seem quite so square to her.

Claudia never traveled alone. Every year she showed up with her lover, and it had never been the same person two years in a row. This year we didn't know what to expect. What neither of us could have guessed was that it would be a young girl in her teens, a young girl with a fixed smile and vacant eyes. Maybe that will be the new trend. Anyway, Sandy was a teen-aged runaway from a Los Angeles suburb and during the week they spent with us, she said scarcely a word. Sometimes she looked as though she might want to speak, but always she thought better of it. Claudia explained that it was the environment, that the suburbs reminded Sandy of her home and intimidated her. She assured us that under the wild New Mexican moon, Sandy was positively voluble.

By this time, the preparation of a company dinner did not seem to be too much of an obstacle. For Claudia and Sandy I was going to serve my latest discovery, my chicken-breast special. It was a recipe that came from no cookbook—just boneless chicken breasts sautéed in butter and lemon and wine and a little used spice, marjoram. After a few minutes, chopped spinach is added and the entire dish is put in the oven.

The two of them had dropped their knapsacks and kicked off their sandals and they were settling in quickly. This was not to deny the difference in our worlds and those first few hours were spent trying to locate a common language and other cultural linkups. We spent that first afternoon together assuring each other how little we had aged, a conversation that had precious little interest for one of Sandy's tender years.

Then it was time to prepare the dinner. They followed me into the kitchen and watched as I dusted the chicken breasts with flour and spices. Sandy seemed anxious to say something. She was tug-

109

ging at Claudia's sleeve in much the manner of a small child trying to capture her mother's attention.

"Oh no," Claudia said. "That looks like chicken."

"Chicken breasts," I said.

"You go ahead," Claudia said. "I don't want you to change a thing, but just don't waste any on us."

"You don't like chicken?" Corinne said.

"Didn't I write you?" she said. "Sandy is a macrobiotic and she's persuaded me that it's the best thing to do. But you go ahead and eat whatever if you want to. We never eat flesh but we'll make do somehow."

"Let me think," I stalled. I was thinking about the other main dish I had planned, a spinach salad with bacon dressing. "We were considering going out to dinner anyway. Why don't we do that?"

"That would be fun," Claudia said. "I haven't been out to a restaurant in a year or so."

I had to think of a restaurant that would not be too hard on a macrobiotic diet and one that would, at the same time, tolerate customers wearing bibbed overalls and sandals. We settled finally on a Chinese restaurant at a nearby shopping center.

During the course of the dinner, Claudia told us what she was "into" this year. She was into brown rice in a big way. She was into the environment. And she was into taking good care of her old lady, as she also put it. Whenever she referred to her that way, as her "old lady," it took me a moment to realize she was talking about Sandy.

"We're going to help you while we're here," Claudia was saying. "Like I can help you with the cooking."

"What cooking?" I said. "I've been sitting here thinking what I can make for you two and all I've come up with so far is a cheese soufflé, my famous noncollapsible soufflé."

"Oh, no eggs," Claudia said. "I mean, we decided you either do something or you don't, and what is an egg except an undeveloped chicken. So we don't eat eggs."

"What do you eat then?"

"Oh, almost anything else," she said.

I tried to think what that might be but could think of nothing.

"What do you cook at home?" I asked.

"Well, my specialty is yin-and-yang vegetable soup," she said.

"In fact, I'll make you my special vegetable soup while I'm here. Can you get okra?"

"I always wondered what you did with okra."

"Tomorrow you'll see," she said. "I'll give you a list of the things I'm going to need and I'm going to make you a vegetable soup that you're not going to believe. The main thing wrong with most other vegetable soups is that they use a beef base. I use an eggplant-and-mushroom base."

"That certainly sounds interesting."

"You'll see," she promised.

As the evening wore on, we discovered that Claudia was also into organic gardening, solar heat, geodesic domes, and all oriental religions. The things she was not into included politics, reading, writing, television. In short, then, we had absolutely nothing in common.

The next morning, as Corinne was getting ready to leave for the office, I was planning a trip to the supermarket. I ripped up my old list and started a new one. I began by writing down "brown rice" and after that I was at a loss.

"I'll go with you," Claudia said. "I can show you what to get."

"I'd love to go along," Corinne said to us, "but there are a million things to do at the office."

Corinne seemed in an unusually gay mood as she left us that morning. I began to understand her gaiety as Claudia and I were driving to the supermarket. She swiveled around in her seat and looked me square in the face as she talked.

"I know Sandy doesn't talk much," she said, "but I can tell she likes you. She trusts you. That means a lot to me. Sandy and I have got a perfect relationship. I've never been able to get it on the way I'm getting it on now."

"That's nice."

I never know how to handle a conversation like that one. But Claudia didn't let my silence bother her. After Sandy, I probably seemed a trifle gabby.

"Sex can be such a beautiful form of communication," she said. "There's nothing like getting it on with someone who really knows where her head is at."

For the first time, Claudia's manner of speech was getting to me. But I didn't say anything and she went on, describing the world's

111

first perfect relationship in much more detail than I cared to know. Never before had I been so anxious to get to a supermarket. But even that offered only brief relief. It became clear that having Claudia with me would result in no economies. She quickly assumed control of the cart and pointed it toward the drug section.

"That soap you folks have been using," she said, "it's a real downer."

The soap that was an upper turned out to be an herbal soap made by the same firm that manufactured the downer. It was definitely an upper in price; the same size bar cost a dollar more.

"That stuff you use would scrape off my skin," Claudia said. "I try not to ever let something unnatural touch my skin."

Claudia's expertise was not limited to soap. She was also expert in tropical fruits, correct brands of sour cream, and dog food. During her stay with us, Claudia took it upon herself to educate us on these important matters. Once she discovered the more expensive vegetable store in Huntington, the supermarket was no longer good enough. And the vegetable store became passé when she found the health-food outlet.

One thing you should know about leading the proper life: bring money. Claudia pointed out, for example, that we could cut down on pollution and energy consumption with the simple installation of a sunlight-heating element on the roof, and the beautiful thing was that it wouldn't cost much over five thousand dollars. And it would be much better for our posture if we had our sandals, or shoes, constructed from individual molds of our feet and that wouldn't cost much more than $140.

Every day as Corinne finished her morning coffee and left, leaving me with Claudia and a young girl who may or may not have been a deaf mute, a feeling of resentment grew in my heart. This, after all, was Corinne's friend, and yet it was I who was providing endless taxi service, I who was learning 101 ways to build meals around mushrooms, I who was suffering.

Before the week came to its unhappy end, I was sneaking away from my home and gorging myself at hamburger stands. Rather than sit home and exchange small talk with Claudia and Sandy, I was spending long, lonely, pleasant hours in the library, reading out-of-date magazines.

112

And all that week Claudia was gathering together the ingredients required for her macrobiotic vegetable soup.

"You've been so nice to us," she said. "It's the least I can do. Oh, wait'll you taste it."

The vegetable-soup dinner went from a small epicurean delight to a banquet. Since Claudia was going to do all the work that Saturday night, she took the opportunity to invite all of her friends, everyone she knew who lived within hitching distance.

And while I must admit that Claudia was appreciative of all my efforts on her behalf, nothing was quite right. They thanked me for laying out the bedclothes—but, well, Sandy couldn't sleep on pillows that full, and the quilt was not down, was it? The mayonnaise, though homemade, had not been made with cold-pressed safflower oil. Our boys' hair was long enough, but not styled properly. The coffee, though made from freshly ground beans, was not Colombian.

The only thing to save me from a breakdown was the fact that Claudia did have other acquaintances in the vicinity. Every morning, after a breakfast I won't try to describe, I taxied the two of them to other unsuspecting souls living in nearby towns.

After a few days, I began to notice that neither Claudia nor Sandy ever lifted a finger around the house. Whenever it became obvious that she should pitch in and help, she talked about that damn macrobiotic soup. She was constantly coming up with new vegetables that I should be keeping an eye out for. For several reasons I was looking forward to the event. It was certainly going to be the high spot of their stay with us. It would be the only night when I didn't have to figure out a dinner to match their dietary habits.

It got to be, finally, Saturday afternoon. I went to the refrigerator and took out all the vegetables I had been accumulating over the week. I laid them out beside the chopping block and made sure that the large soup pot was clean and ready. I knew that any moment now Claudia would come in and begin the slicing and the chopping and the stirring. I was wrong.

"You know," she said, "this is like our last day on the East Coast and there are really some things I'd like to pick up. Do you have time to give us a lift to the shopping center?"

113

"I guess so." Polite to the end. "But how are you going to have time to make the soup before your friends get here?"

"Oh, I hate to lay that whole number on you," Claudia said. "But the stuff's all there and you've just got to throw it in a pot. Like the hard part is just getting the stuff together."

"Claudia . . ."

"I know, I *know*." She didn't. "You're afraid it won't come out the way it would if I was making it. Believe me, it'll be just fine. But if we're going to get there before the stores close, we've got to get a move on. Oh, Michael, don't worry about picking us up. We can hitch back."

I hadn't been worrying about picking her up. I hadn't been worrying about anything except the possibility that I might lose my temper and strangle her. It was time to make a stand.

"But these people who're coming, they're *your* friends."

"Don't worry about that, they'll really dig you."

Corinne had been right. This time I didn't like Claudia. It was the first time I ever had to be a servant to someone outside the family and I have higher ambitions in life than being servant to the world's oldest hippie.

During the drive to the shopping center, I didn't even try to make conversation. On the way home, I made one stop. At the butcher's. For stewing meat. And while our guests were away, I took the meat and browned it and boiled it and simmered it until I had a fine beef broth, the best base for any vegetable soup I knew how to make. Then, ignoring every vegetable I had never seen before, I cut up the onions and the turnips, the cabbage and the carrots.

At five o'clock I removed the bones and the meat from the soup and let the brew simmer. I learned that among Claudia's guests that night were a half-dozen vegetarians, and I felt some guilt toward them—but absolutely none toward Claudia. Just before the dinner hour, after I had greeted all of her friends and done my imitation of a square suburbanite for them, she came breezing in with her arms wrapped around packages. She went directly to the soup pot and took off the lid.

"That smells out-of-sight," she said, mixing her metaphors. I said not a word as she inhaled that rich, deep, dark, hearty beef aroma, and then she took a taste. "Michael! This tastes better than

114

the one I usually make. How did you ever get that marvelous beeflike taste?"

"Worcestershire sauce," I said. "A lot of Worcestershire sauce. And, of course, I used a mushroom-and-eggplant base."

"See," Claudia said, "you hardly needed me at all."

"That's the truth."

"One thing though, what kind of salt are you using. I never use anything except sea salt."

"Of course," I said. "Actually, we don't use just any sea salt. I always insist on salt from the Caspian Sea."

"I had heard about that," Claudia said. "Are you going to serve it the way I told you, with slices of eggplant on top? That's the way I always serve it."

"Claudia, would you stop tasting the soup?"

She gave me a surprised look but backed away nimbly enough. She even helped me dish it out and bring it to the guests. It had been some time since several of them had been that near meat, and while they may have been vegetarians in their heads, they were not vegetarians in their stomachs. Seldom has a simple soup been given such lavish praise. They came back time and time again.

Later, as the kids started to clear away the dishes, I waited to see whether Claudia would offer to help. No, that would have been too much to expect. Ignoring the guests, I got up and helped the kids. Then, while the party progressed without me, I went off to the laundry room and started the machines. Claudia joined me there in the laundry room.

"Everyone is wondering what became of you," she said.

"Oh, I had some work to do."

"You're not going to use the clothes dryer, are you?" she asked.

"That was my intention. Would you like . . ."

"Oh no," she said. "No machine is more wasteful of energy than a clothes dryer. Would you like to know how you can save energy?"

"No."

"No?"

"I have been watching you and Sandy all week and I have a fairly good understanding how people can save energy. Believe me, Claudia, I already know too much about saving energy."

"Well, here's what you have to do. You take a long rope and you run it from the back porch to that tree over there . . ."

"Claudia . . ."

"And then when the clothes are washed, but still wet, you take them out and hang them up on the rope."

"Oh," I said, "it's a device that works very much like a clothesline."

"Precisely."

"Claudia, are you putting me on?"

"Not in the least," she said. "You'd be surprised how much energy is required in using an ordinry clothes dryer. This is really the only thing to . . ."

"Claudia, go back to your guests. Claudia, go anywhere, but go away from me."

The fact that I was laughing at the time may have undercut some of the impact of that message. Nonetheless, Claudia did manage to remove herself from the kitchen with all due speed but with no waste of energy.

I suspected Corinne would be angry at me—and justifiably so. Indeed, after she had time to consider the encounter, Claudia returned and displayed some anger of her own.

"Sandy and I have decided," she said, "to leave earlier than was anticipated."

"Yes?"

"We've decided to catch an early-morning train. The only train leaving at that hour goes from Huntington. I hate to put you out any more on our account, but perhaps it'll be worth it, getting rid of us early."

"Claudia, you're talking to the wrong person."

"Why is that?"

"Tomorrow morning, at whatever hour you settle on, Corinne is the one who'll be driving you to the station. I've been a taxi service long enough for you and . . . Harpo out there. One other thing, since I believe in honesty at any cost, I feel I should tell you that there was meat in that vegetable soup tonight."

That was our last try at conversation. And the following morning, while I slept to an uncharacteristically late hour, Corinne got up to drive our guests to the station. I know it was a violation of our basic agreement, but Corinne seemed not to mind.

116

"Don't you want to say good-by to them?" she said.

"You say good-by for the two of us," I said, "and make it stick."

Again I had failed as a housewife. I had been insufferably rude to one of Corinne's oldest friends. I had made my wife get up at the break of dawn to do something that I should have done. I had been defeated by a job that Corinne had taken in stride every year. As she left me that morning, I had to wonder why she was smiling.

EIGHTEEN

I've never enjoyed a close or abiding relationship with money. I grew up in a solidly middle-class family that never had to do without but, on that precarious trip from one payday to the next, occasionally managed to scrape bottom. Until I went away to school, I didn't realize that there were people who really joined country clubs and purchased Cadillacs and followed the migrating birds south in winter.

Always I was taught that money was not the most important thing in life. The strongest single image I have of my father—I still see him demonstrating the relative unimportance of money by emptying a wallet into a fireplace.

To this day, I feel vaguely uncomfortable if there is too much money on hand. On those few occasions when a savings account has approached five figures, I have taken steps to reduce it at once. I've found it helps if you play the Big Spender role and reach for the tab whenever possible. It also helps if you combine a natural appetite for gambling with a natural love of horses.

For many years I was involved in a neighborhood poker game where the nightly risk could range between five hundred and a thousand dollars. I've visited Las Vegas on gamblers' junkets and while I don't fit many of the gambling stereotypes—I don't own a single set of cuff links—I do enjoy the action. Gambling has never been an expensive hobby, probably because I'm not a compulsive loser. Most of my gambling ventures have shown a tidy profit, possibly because I've always felt free to lose. When a person has a six-hundred-dollar pay check coming in every week, there is no reason to be overly concerned about a thousand-dollar loss.

I had spent the previous three or four years in the constant company of horses. In fact, the year before I had been spending a good part of every day—at least several hours—handicapping the races. Quite frequently I was able to check out my calculations by visiting the track.

Now, for the first time in my life, I had the time to pursue these cultural interests. A weekly poker game would interfere with my housewifely duties—there'd be no way to bounce back from an all-night session and get the kids off to school in proper style. But this would be my year to give the horses the kind of attention they deserve. This year I would be up at the right hour to get the *Racing Form* and then, while the bread was rising or the stew was simmering, those long hours while the children were off at school, I would sit there with slide rule and electronic calculator and prepare myself for the races.

During January and February, while the horses were enjoying the Florida sun, I followed their progress impatiently. I kept up with them as they moved north from Florida to Maryland. This year—ah, this year I would be ready for them.

However, as I was waiting for the horses to arrive, my attitude toward money was going through some changes. This could be attributed to the new economic reality, the fact that money had stopped coming in. I had decided to stay within the hundred-dollar allowance that I received from Corinne every Monday morning, but it was not working out that way. The C-note always seemed to disappear by Wednesday and that happened to be the eve of my big weekly food-shopping trip.

I could have complained, could have asked for a raise in allowance. But I thought back to all those years when Corinne had come to me. The forty-five dollars a week was not enough, she said. The seventy-five was not enough. The ninety was not enough. I could remember being very patient with her, even fatherly, and going over the receipts and adding everything up and showing her that she should have—oh, at least four and a half dollars left over for her own amusements every week.

Undoubtedly, this was the reason she decided early in the marriage to make money on her own. And not until this year did I realize what I had put her through for the weekly pittance. This past history with Corinne made it next to impossible to bring up the subject myself. Instead of coming to her and admitting that it was impossible to make ends meet on the allowance, I started to dip into capital.

This presented problems that were new to me, and my initial reaction was one of confusion. Early in January I started trying to cut corners—having two meatless nights a week, making do with meat loaf for dinner and sandwiches. My own pleasures were modest but even they started to seem expensive. A visit to the pool hall ate up five dollars. A quick stop at the Pier Three, a few rounds with the boys, ate up another five or ten.

It was enough to turn me into a tightwad. Instead of calling an electrician to fix a faulty switch, I figured out how to do it myself. That January our food blender ceased to work. Instead of simply picking up a new one, as I would have done a month earlier, I located the manufacturing company in the wilds of New Jersey, placed a phone call, and wound up sending off for a replacement part. I typed out the order—total cost: $9.15—and handed Corinne the letter as she was leaving for the office.

"Why are you giving me this?"

"It needs a stamp," I said.

"You mean you don't have any stamps? Why didn't you just go out and get some stamps?"

"They cost ten dollars a roll."

"Yes?"

"They cost ten dollars a roll and if I spend that ten dollars, it comes right out of the food budget and that's the price of meat for two meals . . ."

"I'll get you the stamps," she said.

"And I thought you might like to add a check to the envelope."

"Okay."

That little exchange had cost her twenty dollars more than she had planned to spend on that day. By the same token, it had saved me twenty dollars. But it had taken a small toll of each of us.

"By the way," Corinne said, "when are you going to get around to cleaning this place?"

119

By the time three months had gone by, I was fully resigned to dipping into my savings account week after week. Never mind. The horses had been moving steadily northward and were in the neighborhood now. I was just biding my time, waiting for the skies to clear before going out and paying what would surely be the first of many visits.

Although money had become a problem for me, the same was not true for Corinne. Her business was flourishing and she was paying the bills without a murmur of complaint. There was no reason she couldn't give me a cost-of-living raise, but there was no way I could come out and ask her for it. In the old days, when I had wanted a raise from the newspaper, I would leave job offers from rival newspapers where they might be seen by my superiors. I tried a similar approach with Corinne; I began leaving my grocery bills where she might notice them. On Saturday, April 13, I hit a new high—a $63.45 tab from the A&P.

"It's amazing," I said to Corinne, "how the price of food has gone up."

"It *is* amazing," she agreed. "That used to depress me so. In fact, that's probably the thing I miss least of all, shopping at the supermarket. I used to hate it, watching those prices go up week after week."

"Yeah, but the prices are going up now more than they ever did before. I read a story the other day that said even the rate of inflation is rising at a record level."

"I feel sorry for you," she said. "I really would hate to be doing the shopping with that going on."

I decided the hint wasn't quite broad enough.

"You know what's strange, it's strange how that hundred-dollar check hardly pays for the food any more."

"That *is* strange," she said, "especially when you think back to a couple of months ago when you were telling me that hundred dollars would be much more than enough."

I began to sense just how unreasonable I had once been with Corinne. Back when she was doing the shopping, I was convinced that she had taken a lover. That was the only logical explanation. Year after year I had been bringing home the money and suddenly it was no longer enough. Expenses rose ten, fifteen, then twenty

120

dollars a week. I half suspected she was salting away the extra money and supporting some struggling young artist in the city.

Now it was my turn. And as the year wore on, I changed more than a few shopping patterns. As a lifelong Pepsi-Cola freak, I watched the price of a six-pack go from $1.09 to $1.13 to $1.20 in slow, sure increments, and then I stopped buying the stuff. V-8 juice, which happens to mix well with vodka, started at twelve cents for the small can, went to fourteen cents, then finally to sixteen cents before the year was over. First I gave up V-8 juice; by the end of the year I had given up vodka. The economics of being a housewife did some wonderful things for my health.

This was a year of inflation. It became a test of the store owner's ingenuity, and as a close student of the supermarket scene, I had to marvel at the new techniques of price camouflage. The year before the price on the tomato bin had said "Three for $1" and it had meant three pounds. This year it meant three tomatoes. Other stores had started to use a new measure—a "ctn" which was neither a pound nor a tomato but a carton.

Changing the measures is not unlike changing the rules in the middle of the ballgame, but everyone was doing it. The cheese cost ninety-nine cents, the same as it had the year before, but the new container held twelve ounces, not a pound. Mushrooms started appearing in twelve-ounce and eight-ounce boxes. The sign beside the romaine lettuce said "19 cents," the way it always had, but now it was for a pound, not a head.

I began to notice an elevation of language that corresponded to the elevation in prices. Plain old chuck, the kind of meat most at ease in a stew, was now known as "top chuck steak," which was just a way of explaining why it now cost $1.59 a pound. Spare chicken parts, the kind you throw in a soup for added flavor, became a "Southern Fry Combo."

Where it all hit me was at the checkout counter. The items that came to more than $80 halfway through the year would have come to $76.60 the year before, $70 a year before that, $51 five years earlier.

One week, to make the point with Corinne, I compared the food prices in the ads during the years I was paying the bills and during the year she was paying the bills. The increase in prices up to 1969 seemed modest and rational, more than compensated by rising salary scales. Even the rising prices during the first years of this decade seemed reasonable; it was a lazy but distinctively upward spiral. But what was happening during my year as a housewife was something else, something akin to watching a grass fire suddenly hit a dry stand of timber.

Among the foods I abandoned totally: Genoa salami, lox, most cheeses, mayonnaise, all out-of-season fruits and vegetables. Through it all, there were remarkably few bright spots. During the past three decades, bananas had been available at twelve cents a pound. The only other foods available at the same price as the year before were celery and certain brands of cat food. The wise homemaker would obviously want to build the family menu around celery, bananas, and cat food. Anything else was a disaster.

Four months into the year, Corinne added twenty-five dollars to my weekly allowance check. I put up some *pro forma* resistance, but that didn't fool anyone. And now, as in days of old, I felt free to begin the day by picking up the *Racing Form*. I still had not taken the thirty-mile drive to Aqueduct Race Track, but it was almost enough pleasure just to hold the *Racing Form* in my hand. I feel about that publication approximately the same way the average adolescent must feel about *Playboy*.

But what I'm talking about here is not some distant fantasy. I'm talking about a mental exercise that is fully as complicated as—and a thousand times more exciting than—chess. Instead of facing a single opponent, you are matching wits with thirty thousand others. Instead of competing on an even footing, you are asked to begin each bet by giving away 17 per cent in various taxes and levies.

The minute you begin to scan the *Racing Form,* you are involved in both history and biography. This is a Who's Who of horsedom, and there, in agate type, is the life story of every horse running on a given day. One learns of the best moments in that horse's life, the disasters, the background, the age, the capabilities and the condition.

And that is just the beginning. One goes rapidly from history to mathematics. Not just simple math but math that involves slide rules and rotating disks and electronic calculators. Before I am

122

through with the math, I have assigned every horse a separate numerical rating for speed, another for readiness, a third for class.

Once the handicapper has completed the mathematical equations, he enters the discipline of logic. And from there he goes on to less exact sciences, to the area of deductive reasoning, the territory of the dramatist. For what the handicapper must do is prepare a small scenario—he must, as it were, pre-create the race. And, if he has done his work well, he will imagine one—no, two—horses streaking to the fore; he will know which ones lag behind and which ones will have heart in the stretch. He will sense the weights the horses are carrying, feel the distance they are running and, finally, calculate which of the horses will cross the finish line first.

And academic discipline doesn't end with the running of the race. Even then, as the veteran handicapper sits in the stands watching the drama unfold, checking his calculations against reality, he will often fall back on a final academic discipline. For what is needed then, above all else, is a little philosophy.

This year there was one profound difference in my approach toward handicapping. The difference was that this year I was not backing my selections with cash. What was the matter with me? The weather turned balmier, the days softened, and still I delayed. Friends—other newspapermen and horse fanciers—who had joined me in the pursuit of fortune in years past called to make polite inquiries about my health.

I'd like to claim this as a great act of will power, but it was not even a conscious decision. I did not have any idea why I was delaying. Betting on horses was just another thing I was not doing during my year as a housewife. I was not eating at fancy restaurants, I was not buying new clothes, I was not accepting the invitations from Las Vegas hotels, and I was not betting on horses. In very few weeks, without planning the process, I had gone from profligate to monk.

What had I become? I was running around the house turning off faucets and light bulbs. I was putting pennies in Mason jars. I was letting others reach for the bar tab. And the day it all caught up with me, the day of my great rebellion, I was standing, as I so often did these days, in a supermarket checkout line.

I was feeling fairly flush that day. My wallet contained two twenty-dollar bills, the remainder of my weekly allowance, and on this trip I had made no outlandish purchases, nothing remotely extravagant, just a few small items, the mortar connecting the week's two major shopping trips.

Much to my astonishment, the bill came to $37.57. I stood there, thinking it was fortunate that I had not sprung for the sirloin, as I was handed the change and the usual assortment of trading stamps.

A year earlier it had been my custom to take the stamps and hand them to the woman standing behind me in line, airily acknowledging that the collection of these things was beneath my dignity. In recent weeks, like any other housewife, I had been taking the stamps back home, licking them, and putting them into small booklets printed for the purpose of holding the stamps. Once I had gone so far as to study the catalogue, wondering what I might get for my stamps at some future date.

But not on this day. On this day I was thinking about horses running. Horses running unobserved by me. I had spent the morning with my *Racing Form,* and I had discovered a concealed horse in the third, a horse certain to go off at long odds, but a horse who would stand an excellent chance of winning. I looked down at the pitiful amount of change, at those trading stamps, and I thought about licking them and pasting them up in a booklet. No. This time I took the stamps and, before the widening eyes of the checkout girl, I shredded them into tiny fragments.

"But they're *free,*" she protested.

But they're free, the store manager explained to me a few moments later. But they're free, the supermarket executive explained in a letter responding to my formal complaint. But they're free, the shoppers all say.

But they're not free. And what had prompted my small outburst, my moment of high drama in the checkout line, had been a news item in a recent newspaper. Yale University had received a fourteen-million-dollar gift from the trust fund of the late Frederick W. Beinecke. According to the story, this was the largest single gift to the university since a 1970 gift of more than $15 million from another Beinecke, the late Edwin. Much of this money was earmarked for the Beinecke Rare Book and Manuscript Library. And finally, almost as an afterthought, the story mentioned that the Beineckes had amassed their vast fortune through the sale of Green Stamps.

While I have nothing against dazzling displays of business acumen, and even less against magnanimous philanthropic gestures, I cannot shake this image of thousands—no, millions—of housewives patiently licking away at hundreds upon hundreds of trading stamps so that some unformed nineteen-year-old Yale sophomore could have the pleasure of reading Chaucer in the original.

The assumption that women have nothing better to do with their time than count up stamps, lick them, paste them into booklets, preserve them, carry them over to a redemption center where they can be traded in on the latest Teflon-coated geegaw—it was such a monumental insult to intelligence that I wondered why we shoppers ever put up with it.

And, of course, the insult was only a small portion of the price we pay. Someone, after all, has to pay for the paper, the glue, the ink; someone has to pay for the printing presses, the booklets, the catalogues, the dispensing machines; someone has to pay for the redemption centers, the personnel. Someone has to pay for those rare books up at Yale.

The great majority of trading-stamp transactions are undertaken by women. There is a reason for this. Men have, through the years, learned to accept a reward commensurate with their labor; they have learned the value of time. Anyone who understands these things will see the whole collecting-licking-pasting process about as meaningful as playing with paper dolls.

The day of the trading-stamp rebellion, I received a hand-written note from an old classmate. I had, during this time of limited income, ignored all the typewritten pleas for assistance from the school which, ironically enough, was Yale. The handwritten note was real chummy: "How about sharing a little of your success with Yale?"

Well, that year there was no success to share with anyone. That was the year I went to the medical societies of two counties to protest doctor bills. That was the year I learned how to hem and haw when an old friend tried to hit me for a modest loan.

What would happen to me finally? Would I become a wizened old miser? Would I become the kind of person who jots down the

125

mileage figures in a loose-leaf notebook, the kind of person who carries a small calculator into the supermarket with me, the kind of person who goes to the men's room just before the bill arrives?

"Come on, gang," I called to the kids, "we're going to the races."

NINETEEN

As the children gathered together windbreakers and spare change, I looked at the *Racing Form* more closely. How had the favorites been finishing? Who were the hot jockeys, the winning trainers? What post position was favored at what distances?

It would be my first opportunity to use the binoculars given to me by my newspaper cohorts at my good-by party. I picked up a handful of felt-tipped pens, a different color for each set of calculations, and I went back to the calculator for a final run-through.

It began to feel like old times. There was the familiar rush of adrenalin. As I began to put together the calculations, the kids stood around and kibitzed. To what can I compare the moment? The old pro was coming out of retirement—old brown eyes was back. For a moment, just a moment, I felt flickers of doubt, but then it began to come back. It was not the same as in years past—there was a time when my fingers flew over the calculator buttons—but the end results were the same. I couldn't hope to explain the feeling to someone who has not done it, no more than I can explain the satisfaction of doing a crossword puzzle or figuring out a complicated mathematical problem.

"What race are you on now, Dad?"

That, too, was a question from the past and there is a certain hum to it, an impatience, a desire to get on with it. The three children had come to the track with me often enough to know the possibilities. They know, as do I, that it is possible to come from the track a few hundred dollars richer than when you started. They know that it's possible we'll stop on the way home and load up on Cokes and hot dogs and maybe flowers for their mother.

126

This prospect is in our minds as my multicolored jottings begin to crowd the pages of the *Form.*

"What race now, Dad?"

"The eighth." I stood up. "And this'll be the last one. We won't bother to stay for the ninth. If we're not ahead by that time, the horses just won't be trying."

My bravado was slightly forced. The calculations had taken me much longer than they once did. And even as I completed the math work, there were lingering questions. Would last year's system work this year? Was it still too early in the year for the system? Are there too many first-time starters, too many young horses, too many improbables? Had too many long shots been coming in? Did I know what the hell I was doing?

Pondering the possibilities is what elevates handicapping beyond science to art. While I had chosen a probable winner in each of the races, many of them seemed too close to call. There was, in fact, only one absolutely clear choice on the entire card. My plan of action was to bet the other races lightly, saving my resources to back the sure winner, a horse named Johnny Flame, a horse that could not lose his race under any save the most suspicious of circumstances.

During the long, pleasant ride to the track, my three young betting companions held my calculations up against their own. Their equations were slightly more complex than my own, involving such intangibles as the color of the silk, the number of the horse and the name of the owner.

Although the ride to a race track is always pleasant, I was aware this year of many small differences. The main difference: on other years I would have started the day by cashing a pay check.

"Today," I said, "we're going to go easy. Just two dollars every race."

"Two dollars?" Sean said. "You'll never make it."

"Nope, that's it—two dollars and no more, unless we're ahead."

Sean gave me one of his looks. Diamond Sean McGrady, last of the big spenders. Ah, but I've always been a source of embarrassment to Sean. The clothes I wear. The dented old Volkswagen we drive. And I got still another uplifted eyebrow from Sean when we headed toward the grandstand instead of the clubhouse.

"I guess we're not getting free tickets this year," he said.

By the time we were settled, it was too late to bet on the first race. There was just time to watch the field of horses as they rounded the first turn and swept into the stretch. I tried out the new binoculars and they were a thing of joy even though they were focused on my carefully considered choice finishing well behind the leaders.

"Okay," Sean said, "we just saved two dollars on that race and that means we can bet four dollars on the next one."

"I don't know," I said. "I think we ought to save the two dollars and put it all on Johnny Flame—that's the only horse I'm sure about."

Yes, that was sound strategy. I picked up the *Form* again and was reassured to observe that Johnny Flame had finished first in each of his previous four outings, and today, for some not easily discernible reason, he was running against a distinctly inferior breed of animal.

The winning gambler, I have learned, is the one who stays true to his betting blueprint and resists the deadly lure of the impulse. Show me the bettor who attempts to counter a losing streak or extend a winning streak by suddenly betting heavily, and I will show you a born loser. On this day, I had decided to bet no more than two dollars on the uncertain races, and it was a sound plan. I do not recall ever having been so consistently wrong. It was not just that my choices were being nosed out. No, my horses all ran like hobbyists—they bumped into railings, knocked against other horses, seemed generally determined to finish well out of the money.

By allowing the children to invest a dime in each of my bets, I sold them a small share of the disaster. I could see that they were starting to lose their faith, but that's not what bothered me the most. What was truly bothering me was that I was soon down twelve dollars. What would that do to my budget next week? Maybe I could talk Corinne into taking us all out for pizza one night. Maybe I could give up my pool game for the week. When Liam asked me if he could have a hot dog, I found myself debating the issue—hmm, I wonder how much a hot dog costs this year.

No wonder I was losing race after race. The one way to guarantee a loss is to need to win. I've never seen anyone gamble properly under that kind of pressure. There I was, sitting in the grand-

128

stand instead of the clubhouse, harboring pennies from one race to the next, debating the wisdom of purchasing a frankfurter—naturally I was losing. Even if I were winning I'd be losing.

My first move, after coming to this realization, was to take the kids to the nearest restaurant, lead them up to the counter, and cut them loose: "Anything you want, gang." While they took full advantage of the change in pattern, I went to an adjacent bar for a double dose of Jack Daniel's. It cost $2.50. Better, much better. And coming up, a horse named Johnny Flame and a race he could not lose.

This time I walked past the bustle of the two-dollar windows, past the long lines of losers who lived their lives in such surroundings. Peasants. I strolled past all the six-dollar combination windows, past the ten-dollar and the fifty-dollar windows. I found myself back in the old neighborhood, the hundred-dollar betting window. The line there was understandably small, and there was no jostling, no other evidence of economic anxiety. Not only was there no delay in placing the bet, there seemed to be a flow of unstated respect between the ticket seller and the patron. I put down the hundred. Johnny Flame to win. For the first time all day, I began to feel relaxed.

The horses came out of the paddock and were paraded in front of the grandstand and at that moment I noticed one little detail that I had neglected to consider in my handicapping. This super horse, this unbeatable steed, this Johnny Flame, had been given 122 pounds to carry, while the other horses in the race were carrying 109 pounds each.

Why hadn't I noticed that before? The weight would surely make a difference over the distance of a mile and an eighth. I could see this was going to be a closer race than anticipated. Oh, my horse would win all right—but it would not be a runaway. The appearance of the horse was reassuring. There are things to look for—the sheen of the coat, the way the head is held, the ball-bearing motion of the hips—and on every count, Johnny Flame was a beautiful animal, a worthy son of the splendid Stage Door Johnny.

And he was every bit as good as he looked. He ran one of those adrenalin-generating races, a near faultless come-from-behind effort. He swept past other horses as though they were running in slow motion, and despite all the extra weight, he was heading for the lead as the pack rounded the last turn. Passing less worthy animals with every stride, Johnny Flame came right up to the front and finished a very close second.

"Let's go home," I said.

"Okay," Sean said.

It was a silent ride home. No stops for hot dogs and Cokes, no flowers for the waiting wife. We turned on the radio and listened to a recreation of the race that we had walked out on, the eighth from Aqueduct. Of course, we had not bet that race. Of course, our selection—an eleven-to-one long shot—finished first. It was a small consolation, such a small consolation that our first day of racing this year was also our last.

TWENTY

"I want to see a dirty movie," Corinne said.

"No you don't," I said.

"Shouldn't that be my decision?"

"Believe me, those movies were not meant to be seen by women."

"I want to see one anyway—you have."

She was right. In recent years I had managed to find a way to write columns about such hard-core classics as *Deep Throat* and *The Devil in Miss Jones* and *Behind the Green Door*. But this had been part of my job, essential to keeping abreast of our times. But I had always been reluctant to expose Corinne to this side of our culture.

Corinne, however, persisted. A deal is a deal; a trade is a trade; whatever I had done in the past, she could do in the present. So, one day in September she led me to the Manhattan movie theater showing *The True Adventures of Xaviera Hollander*. A blown-up review posted in front of the theater pointed out that this would be an excellent place for Corinne to begin: "If you are going to see one porno movie this year, or if this is your first porno movie, go see this one."

130

"Okay," I said. "But this is it. After we see this one, I don't want to talk about it again."

"What if I like it?" she said.

Before going in, before committing ourselves to the five-dollar tickets, I read the entire review. The male lead was not described as handsome or artistic or dramatically effective. No, the reviewer had not used any of the more common theatrical phrases in describing the male lead. He was described as "massively endowed."

"I think there's a better movie over on the next block," I said to Corinne.

"What's wrong with this one?"

"Oh, nothing," I said. "It's just that this other one is supposed to be much better."

The next movie we came to, *Teenage Stepmother,* had no glowing reviews out front and Corinne looked at me with suspicion. Waiting for no further hesitation on my part, she walked courageously up to the box office to buy the tickets. She got *some* look from the woman selling tickets. If Corinne had been dressed in leather and carrying a whip, she would have gotten the same kind of look. But Corinne did not appear to be particularly flustered as she handed the woman the exact price of admission, two five-dollar bills, and took the tickets. Then she waited for her change.

"Come on," I said.

"I'm waiting for my change."

"There ain't no change, honey," the ticket-seller said. "That's what it cost."

As I followed Corinne through the small but crowded lobby, I tried to ignore the startled glances from other patrons. The theater itself was crowded and we stood at the back, peering through the smoke, trying to locate two empty seats together. Up near the front there seemed to be two adjacent spaces, but I was not about to parade Corinne past a full house of males. I was spared that indignity when a gentleman gave up his in the back row.

The time had come to look up at the movie screen. It seemed to be a movie about an earthquake. I could make out mountains trembling and a volcano; then the camera backed up and we were able to determine that it was not an earthquake after all. The heaving pink landscape turned out to be a collection of young women throwing themselves at a young man who had procreative apparatus that he would have had trouble supporting without help, a challenge he did not have to meet in the course of the movie.

"I wonder what his face looks like," Corinne whispered after a while.

It was a question not immediately answered. However, when his face was finally revealed, one could understand the director's reluctance to emphasize it.

The story line itself was not what one would describe as complicated: boy meets girls, boy gets girls, boy meets more girls, and so forth. Nor was the film burdened with any heavy "messages" or solemn dialogue. The most interesting exchange took place when a naked man is seen peeking through a window at one of the orgies in progress. He is approached by a young girl wearing overalls and a plaid shirt.

"Whatchagot there?" she says.

"Ah, nothin'."

"Can I look?"

"Nah."

"It's okay, I'm a bird-watcher."

"Ah, I guess so," he says.

"Can I touch it?"

"Okay," he says.

Those are just the first of many suggestions she makes, some of them downright ingenious. She is the kind of girl my mother has always described as "common." Well, I was starting to get interested in the story, but by this time Corinne was having difficulty restraining her giggles. There is nothing quite so disconcerting as a giggle at the wrong moment and some of the customers were turning around to throw a glare in our direction.

"We can leave now," Corinne finally said. "I've seen all that I want to."

"Ah, it's just getting good."

And so it was that we learned not all roles can be reversed, not all experiences are interchangeable.

TWENTY-ONE

Like some latter-day sci-fi character, I am forever wandering into wrong worlds. I walk into a store and the salesman will be wearing one of those cute jackets with the pinched waists and his hair will be hot-brushed over his ears and he will be studying my necktie with some amusement. Last year's width. Well, I have gotten too old to run from these places, so I try to brave it out. I ask if he carries suspenders and he says yes, of course he carries suspenders. And I say please show me suspenders with clips and he says, oh, he doesn't carry those . . . ah . . . clip-on suspenders. It is this kind of experience that ruins shopping for most men, and personally, I would as soon get teeth filled or drink sweet wine or climb mountains.

And there is this one other factor that I might mention in passing, one other reason why many people do not enjoy shopping. It is associated in their minds with the sudden disappearance of rather large sums of money.

But this year there would be no way to avoid it. Not if the children were going to be given such amenities as clothing and shoes. Since Corinne had always done this job in the past, it was now my assignment. I avoided it as long as possible but I got my on-the-job training one Tuesday late in April.

Siobhan needed a new pair of slacks. Since this was to be my first shopping trip for the family, Corinne agreed to meet us at the shopping center and serve as a guide. The shopping center itself was a masterpiece of small artificial comforts—plastic tropical trees, controlled temperature, fountains glowing green and yellow, a mechanical river running under a small bridge arching from nowhere to nowhere, the interminably upbeat music.

It was a comfortable setting for middle-class suburbia, everything modish but not extreme, practical but not pinchpenny. There are weekly exhibits—customized dune buggies one week, mobile homes the next—that bring our materialistic fantasies to life. This particular week the display was of boats and I was stopped by a lacquered crimson GTX Winner, a "sharkline" speedboat with a sixty-five-horsepower motor, black with silver streaks.

Siobhan led us past all this splendor to the department store. We went to the second floor, to the Junior Miss Department and directly to the Awful Taste Division. My newly discovered practical nature immediately exerted itself as I tried to interest Siobhan in the wide selection of jeans.

"Oh, Daddy, not those!"

"Why not?"

"Well, I'm not a farmer."

Not so easily dissuaded, I tried to point her toward the most fashionable jeans, the pre-fades and flares and so forth, but my efforts were greeted by one of those witheringly judgmental glances that will someday be the undoing of men other than her father. Then she made a beeline for the kind of slacks she had in mind all alone. The style might fairly be described as updated zoot-suit—too full in the legs, super-thin belt, speckled material, wide cuffs. All for thirteen dollars, more money than her father had ever in his life paid for a pair of slacks.

"Tell me just this one thing," I said. "What in the hell's the matter with the dungarees we were just looking at? They cost five dollars less."

"You can buy them if you like," she said. "The only thing is I won't wear them."

I stood there, a model of powerlessness, as my daughter prepared to costume herself in the manner of some comic-book character. Where was Corinne anyway? Siobhan walked into the fitting room with a half-dozen slacks under her arm and she reappeared every few moments to show me the latest aberration. The other shoppers in the department were, without exception, mother-daughter combinations, and once again I felt like an intruder. The mothers were much more tolerant of bad taste than I could ever be, and at times I felt I would drown in a sea of "How adorables!" Whenever I issued one of my opinions—"That's humorous" or "Eccchhhhh!"—the other parents would shoot a look at me: what's *he* doing here? Corinne finally appeared to rescue me.

"Can I do anything?" she asked.

"Stop her," I said, "stop her before she buys anything."

"Well, let me try to help out."

While Corinne took over, I slipped across the store to pick up a pair of trousers for Liam. Liam is not easy to fit, but, all in all, it took me approximately three minutes to find the trousers and complete the purchase. I returned to the Junior Miss department just as Siobhan came out of the dressing room wearing slacks that seemed to be manufactured of canvas and rhinestones.

"No," I whispered to Corinne.

"Don't worry," she whispered back.

"I like this one," Siobhan said.

"Yes, I see what you mean," Corinne said. "That's just the kind of thing the younger girls are wearing. They make you look so cute and young, just like a little girl again."

"Oh?"

So much for the canvas-and-rhinestone slacks. Oh, there are things about being a mother that I am never going to learn. At this point, I retired from the scene, defeated once again by a task the most housewives seem to take for granted. As I was leaving the store, I saw one woman suddenly turn and cuff a child in a stroller. This year I saw that same scene often enough in stores and in markets to begin to understand why it takes place. For many women, shopping represents a rare excursion into a predominantly adult world, and there is no reminder of reality more vivid than a child in a stroller.

I waited beside my dog, Lester, in the parked car while Corinne and Siobhan completed their transaction. They came out finally with one of the pairs of jeans that I had admired in the first place.

"How did you manage that?" I asked Corinne.

"Oh, it's just that you've got the wrong attitude," she said. "It was fun."

To this day, I fail to understand how anyone can get pleasure from the act of shopping. During the first week of the year, Corinne gave me a full set of department-store credit cards, eight of them in all. I tried using them, but it took great effort. I used one of them to buy a sweater and I have not worn that sweater since then. Nor have I used a department-store credit card a second time.

During the early years of marriage, when it became necessary for her to escape the house and the drudgery, Corinne would often chart an escape route through the nearest department stores. She has always been a frugal shopper, one who would travel hours in search of a bargain. Later, the escape to the stores became a once-a-week social pastime done in the company of a close friend. The two of them would tour the most fashionable stores and occasionally even make a purchase, though the purchase was by no means an essential part of the trip.

Then, just a couple of years ago, the zing went out of this for her. As she became more and more involved with her business, she became less content with the weekly shopping excursion.

I once talked this over with feminist Gloria Steinem and she said this progression was a not uncommon occurrence. Shopping, after all, holds a clear edge over such other housewifely pastimes as spoon-feeding infants or changing diapers. It is an area where mature women are permitted to make a decision. To buy or not to buy—at least it's a question.

"It *is* a question," she said. "The only power women have in this country is purchasing power, the power of the consumer. Most women are so thoroughly trained to be consumers that they can't get over it . . . But the world of the store is anti-feminist. And now I hate to go shopping. The more I'm involved with life, the more I'm doing, the more separated I am from my desire to buy new things. It's clearly a feminist problem—we've always been treated as objects and we've always defined ourselves by the acquisition of new things."

The role of househusband was new enough so that I had no idea how I would be defined, but it would never be through the acquisition of new things. Through this year I have tried to shop, have bought clothes for the kids whenever it was necessary, but never took an ounce of pleasure from the process. The fact that I don't like shopping hardly places me in a unique category. Surely there are many who take to it the way I do, which is about the way a duck takes to oil.

TWENTY-TWO

One day near the end of the year, my youngest child had an announcement to make. He waited until we were all seated around the dinner table and then Liam sprang it on me.

"No one knows you any more," he said.

"What do you mean by that?" Corinne asked.

"No one ever asks me any more if I'm Mike McGrady's son," he explained. "All my teachers used to ask me that. Now they don't even know who you are."

Over the year I had heard that announcement in many forms. If, as has been observed, fame is fleeting, then local fame is as transitory as summer lightning. Losing an identity was in some ways like losing an anchor; for a time I felt adrift, floating, but after more time, I began to appreciate that feeling. For the first time in many years I was not pigeonholed; people didn't know me before they met me.

That is not to say I didn't miss the job. I did. I missed the pace and the people. Ironically, during the first months away from the newspaper, I was besieged by column ideas. They jumped out at me from every corner, they woke me up in the middle of the night, they competed with each other for a spot in my mind.

For a while I would call up other columnists and try to pass along the ideas. But ideas are not easily transplanted, and eventually I stopped calling and started writing the columns in the privacy of my mind. Oh, I wrote some beautiful mental columns this year, but it was just not the same.

Nor did it help matters when *Newsday* delayed in naming a successor. Every time I looked at my old page in the newspaper, the page I had deserted, I felt a pang. Finally the paper selected an old friend and colleague, Stan Isaacs, to fill the space, and Stan immediately called to suggest that we have lunch. I must have felt akin to a divorced man meeting his former wife's new mate; not until then did everything seem final. It was a pleasant lunch, but the experience left me feeling glum.

The glumness continued later that same day when I met another colleague, columnist Pat Owens, for our regular game of pool. Pat told me he was off for Washington, D.C., on the morrow, a two-week excursion through the latest political scandal. I couldn't quite conceal my disappointment at the news. In the first place, it meant that I was going to have to do without my pool game for the next two weeks. A small thing? Not to me; it was one of the few pastimes I had managed to carry over, intact, from one life to the next. It also happened to be one of the few things I was doing that year that wasn't a crashing bore.

If I had still been at *Newsday*, I, too, might be packing a bag, grabbing a plane, covering a big story. With no difficulty at all, I could conjure up the scene in Washington. The city, crowded with media stars and camp followers, would have a festival atmosphere. I imagined the late-night, whiskey-laced conversations, the reporters flying in from all over the country while I slept quietly in Northport, conserving my strength for another day of cleaning and cooking and caring for the family.

After the pool game, as we were sliding onto our stools at the Pier Three, I looked up above us and there, taped to the bar mirror, staring down, was an eight-by-ten photograph of the man who was then seated beside me. Roger, the owner of the Pier Three, had started a gallery of celebrity photographs, pictures of his famous customers. He had begun by putting up the picture of the only political columnist to frequent the bar and so far that was the sum total of his celebrity gallery. Not too long ago, my picture would have been up there, too—but that was back at the same time it was running three times a week in the newspaper. Roger seemed to be reading my mind.

"Hey, Mike, why don't you bring us a picture?" he said. "We could put it right up there beside Pat's."

Nothing serves to aid the cause of depression more than well-intentioned charity. Roger's overly generous invitation ignited a mental chain-reaction. Once the picture was up, what then? What would the barmaids say when new customers asked them to identify the photograph. They would have to reach. "Oh, he was once . . ." or "Oh, he used to . . ." Whatever they would say, it would be in the past tense.

This was going to be one of those days. The drinker two bar-

138

stools down the line identified Pat Owens from his picture. I sensed that he may have been a steady reader. I sensed that because he looked as though he'd like to throw a punch, and that is the kind of column Pat writes.

"And what've you been up to, McGrady?" He looked as though he still might want to throw a punch; I guess he read my column as well. "What've you been up to since you left the rag?"

How many times did I hear that question throughout the year? There was nothing wrong with the question except my inabilty to answer it.

"Nothing," I said.

"Nothing?"

"He's just being modest," Pat came to my defense.

What sometimes passes for modesty is a realistic appraisal of the situation. Whenever the subject of me came up, I had problems. The way I was spending my days was not something you could talk about in a saloon; it was something you would forget.

"Hiya, boys, how's it going?"

Fred, a widower and recently retired telephone lineman, managed to rescue me. Fred was a regular at the saloon up the road. Since his retirement, however, he had taken to moving around restlessly from one bar to another, making his rounds as diligently and predictably as a postman. After a few moments of talk, he got up and toddled on down the road toward the next tavern.

"It's a shame how Fred has disintegrated since leaving the phone company," Pat observed.

"I hadn't noticed that."

"Well, he has," Pat said. "It's pitiful what has been happening to him. The way he rambles on for hours now, repeating himself, forgetting the point to the story. He has become a caricature of himself and it's a sad thing to see."

This line of talk didn't do a hell of a lot for my mood. Was Pat trying to say something? Was he implying that all men who left their jobs disintegrated into Jello-headed bores? Had I been talking too much, rambling, offering him evidence of some similar disintegration. I looked at the clock and got up to leave; I explained that I had to get home early because a batch of dough was on the rise.

Later, putting the loaves in the oven and trying not to think about the piles of laundry on the floor, I couldn't help but think of Pat flying off to Washington. I imagined him at the airport, then at the ticket counter, then on the plane ordering a tall drink from the stewardess, all ordinary scenes infused with new glamour. Compared to the life I was leading, it was as though he were boarding the Orient Express.

I was saved from my mood by the unexpected arrival of another friend from the newspaper. Dan had stopped at the house to deliver an accumulation of press releases, and he stayed on for a drink and then another.

"How're things at the office?" I asked.

"That place is some mess," Dan said. "I'm telling you, they have some troubles now. I've never seen morale so bad before. Just terrible. But I didn't come over here to complain about the job—how're you?"

"First, tell me about the paper," I said. "And don't leave out any of the bad stuff."

Dan took me at my word. For the better part of a fifth of Bourbon, he sat there and unraveled a tale of office politics, petty jealousies, widespread executive incompetence, disastrous office romances, stories of intrigue and infighting that would have curled a lesser man's hair. It was just what I wanted to hear. Once one is removed from the battlefield, one tends to remember the heroism and forget the carnage. At times it is good to be reminded of the carnage. Otherwise, one might return to the battlefield.

It was never what you would call an identity crisis. During many previous leaves of absence, I had learned about the shortness of memory of even the most ardent admirer and I realized that the old label, columnist, was simply a convenience for the benefit of people who didn't know you as anything else. But the new identity, househusband, required endless explanation, and by year's end, I was skirting the issue whenever it came up.

Sometimes it could not be avoided. One Saturday in autumn, following a shopping spree at a new A&P supermarket, I found myself short of cash. It made sense to obtain check-cashing privileges and I went back to the customer-service booth and outlined the situation to the youthful assistant manager.

"What do you do for a living?" he asked.

"My wife is president of her own firm."

"And you," he said, "what is your place of employment?"

"This may sound strange to you," I said, "but I'm the housewife and my wife is the breadwinner. She's the one who makes the living and I'm the one who takes care of the house."

"I'm not sure what to do about this," he said. "Is your wife here?"

"No, she's home today."

"Listen," the young man said, "I'll cash a check for you today, but no greater than the amount of the order. I'll give you this form and you can take it home and ask your wife to fill it out."

No one could accept the switch at face value. Time and again I was asked what I was *really* doing that year. Some wondered whether I was still paying the bills or whether Corinne was still doing some of the cooking. To men, it was the sacrifice of a precious birthright. To women, it was insanity.

Occasionally people would stop in with no apparent reason other than to see whether we were living up to the agreement. One neighborhood friend Allison stopped by early on a November afternoon and seemed surprised to learn that Corinne was really at the office and I was really at home. She stayed for a cup of tea.

"Are you enjoying it so far?" she asked.

"It?"

"Being the woman of the house."

"It's not so bad," I said. "Even this, for example—in my old life I was never able to knock off whenever I wanted to for a cup of tea."

"I really didn't believe Corinne would still be at the office," Allison said. "And she does go there every day."

"She hasn't missed a day," I said. "How do you take your tea?"

"Oh, let me," she said.

"No," I said, "I can handle it."

Making tea is not what you would call an enormous challenge, but judging from the expression in Allison's eyes, I could have been whipping up a little charlotte russe. Allison, married sixteen years and the mother of three, had definite difficulty in accepting the switch.

"Everyone always asks me what you're doing," she said.

"Everyone?"

"Just everyone," she said. "I've told them you're working on a secret novel."

"That's what you've told them?"

"Yes," she said, "how is your writing going?"

"What writing?"

"Oh, come off it," she said. "Are you trying to tell me that you're just staying home and doing *nothing?*"

"You've been doing this for sixteen years and you call it nothing?"

"I have been doing it for sixteen years," Allison said, "and that's why I feel free to call it nothing."

Throughout the year I didn't meet a woman who understood why I was doing it. They looked at me the way a lifer might look at an innocent person trying to break into prison. They knew something I didn't know. And as the year crept along, I began to feel the need for new outlets. Cooking could be creative but it had its limits. I may well have missed the wider applause; I know I missed cashing a pay check. Whatever the reason, I sought out excuses to write and I found the simple act of sitting in front of a typewriter for an hour or two in the morning made the rest of my day more tolerable. I began by writing a spoof of a popular record, then a couple of short pieces. I took to writing letters and speeches for a local political candidate. And by the end of the year, more as a game than as a serious literary effort, I was co-writing a novel with Harvey Aronson, a successful writer and friend of long standing. This meant getting up at five in the morning and stopping at nine to again become a housewife.

My total income for the year was less than three thousand dollars, but I was, for once, not working for money. I was working because it was absolutely necessary. And there was this added bonus: when someone asked me what I was doing for a living, I could say, "Oh, I'm a writer."

At this writing, now that I am no longer a househusband, I feel I may have overreacted to diminished status. After all, the only people who confuse an occupation with a person's identity are people who don't really know the person. If we have to worry about impressing strangers, then we're to be pitied.

What did it all mean anyhow? At the end of the year, in the

twelfth month of the switch, we were in a celebratory mood one night and reserved a table at a brand-new restaurant in town. The table was reserved under the name McGrady, a name that once ensured the best table in the house. In many respects, that night reminded me of the old days. The table *was* excellent and the service was impeccable and the food was marvelous.

"See," Corinne pointed out to me, "everything is perfect and they have no idea who you are. It's possible for people to treat us nicely and not be angling for some mention in the newspaper."

She spoke too soon. As we were leaving the restaurant, the owner and his wife suddenly materialized by the door. I have seldom been granted such broad smiles, such warm handshakes.

"It's been an honor having you here," the owner said.

"Oh, it's been our pleasure," Corinne said.

"Yes, I always read your column," the owner said. "It's my favorite column and I never miss it."

"Yes," his wife said, speaking a year after the appearance of my farewell column, "every night we race to the paper to see what you're writing about that day."

"It's always nice," I said, "to meet close readers."

TWENTY-THREE

I've always been close to the two boys. Boys play basketball and pool, and it has not been difficult to be one of those pal-fathers with them. Siobhan has not so easily tolerated my clumsy displays of affection. She is a proper girl and I am something of an oaf, a large-sized creature who is forever trying to hug her in supermarket aisles, a constant source of embarrassment who flirts outrageously with all of her thirteen-year-old girl friends.

This year there have been opportunities to get closer to Siobhan, and I have cherished every one of them. We have gone shopping together, run errands together, visited the orthodontist together, even had a conversation or two. She has demonstrated the New Math to me while I have argued the merits of the Old Math to her. As she has come to know the oversized male who lives in her

143

house, she has even discussed a problem or two with me, and since I was the sole remaining at-home adult, I have even helped her with her homework from time to time.

"Daddy, I have to give a talk in Public Speaking tomorrow. And I *hate* to give talks."

"I'm glad that you brought the matter up," I said. "This happens to be an area I've had some experience in."

My experience had come the previous year when Sean had gone through the same course. The specific assignment—prepare and deliver a talk of persuasion—was one I had worked out with Sean a year earlier. As luck would have it, we had come up with an idea that had merited him an A-plus. It was the same assignment and a different teacher; there seemed no reason why she couldn't adopt the same idea to her own uses.

This was the basic concept: Siobhan was going to attempt to persuade her classmates to eat a candy bar. The way this was to be done, as she was delivering the talk she was to unwrap a large milk chocolate bar and very slowly devour the candy in front of the class. Together, we scripted the talk. "This candy bar tastes like . . . (take mouthful) . . . ummmm, tastes like . . . (take mouthful) . . . tastes . . . very good. The texture is, ummmm . . . (take mouthful) . . . the texture is, ah . . . (take mouthful) . . . the texture is very smooth."

And so on. A million laughs, right? Wrong. The same basic talk that had, the year before gotten an A-plus, this year got a D. The teacher had even gone to the trouble of writing Siobhan a brief critical appraisal that, in its entirety, said, "This is the worst cop-out I've ever seen."

"That's all he had to say."

"No, that's all he had to write," Siobhan said. "He had some other things to say. He said he didn't like the idea of anyone eating candy in front of the class."

"But that was the point; that was the joke."

"I don't think he has a very good sense of humor."

It was the first time in seven years of lower education that Siobhan had gotten a grade as low as a D. Not coincidentally, it was also the first time she had ever really let me help her with the homework. She tried to shrug it off, but she was taking it more

144

seriously than she admitted. At the dinner table I noticed her eyes were suddenly full and she was having some trouble swallowing.

"Eat up all your dinner, young lady," I warned her, "or I'll never help you with your homework again."

In time—it took a week or two—Siobhan did allow me to help her with her homework again but never again did she ask for assistance in Public Speaking.

After all those years of seeing the children only at the dinner table, it was a strange sensation to be close with them. Perhaps this is best seen as a mixed blessing but I know that I was looking forward to their first vacation every bit as much as they were. One of the drawbacks of this new life, one I had not anticipated, was the built-in loneliness. Moreover, with the kids at home, I wouldn't have to get up at dawn to pack lunches and make breakfasts. I would sleep late and when I got up, there would be people to talk to, company, conversation.

"I'm bored," Sean said on the first day. On the second day he woke up and said, "There's nothing to do around here." Thereafter he varied it slightly: "What's there to do around here?" Occasionally, Liam would have a comment: "There's nothing to eat around here."

Needless to say, they found something to do over the vacation. What these three bright, engaging, vigorous children did, they did what they always do during vacations; they disintegrated.

Where they did their disintegration was generally in the vicinity of a television set. They would sit there motionless except for commercial breaks, then they ate. What that meant was that they were eating approximately ninety-one meals a day. Next time I'll get a refrigerator with a revolving door. Occasionally, whenever the violence level fell, they would take a break from television and methodically dismantle the house. The way this worked, I am convinced, is that each child selected a specific target area—say, a living room or a kitchen—at the beginning of the day and if that area was not a shambles by the end of the day, then that child had failed.

Although I knew it to be a losing proposition, I tried during the vacation to direct their attention toward the printed word. Failing that, I'd settle for any serious television program. At the end of

145

every day I attempted to pry them away from cartoons and introduce them to the news programs. One night we were seated there watching the news and it was an unbroken series of disasters. A graphic ten-minute film on famine in Africa. Earthquakes in Chile. Terrorists in Lebanon. Murder in London. In light of all this, Liam had an eminently sensible question.

"Dad, is Ford President of the *whole* world?"

This turned out to be one of the easier questions I had to handle. The main staple of the television season that vacation seemed to be the subject of rape. There was hardly a series that didn't have at least one major rape episode, and one observer counted more than a hundred prime-time rapes over the season. I should hardly have been surprised when Liam's entirely normal curiosity could no longer be contained.

"Dad, what is rape anyhow?"

That was the kind of question their mother had been handling for years. The way she handled these queries was entirely admirable—she was honest, clinical, thorough. When she finished her answer to a question like that, the matter had been cleared up once and for all. I asked myself: what would Corinne say? She might explain that rape was when a man tried to have a baby with a woman who didn't want to have the baby. No, she would go further, probably even addressing herself to such areas as penetration and forcible entry. Corinne has the kind of mind that does not shy away from the pertinent detail, even the sordid aspect.

"Rape," I explained to Liam, "is sexual assault."

"Oh," he said.

Beautiful. There were no follow-up questions and I was just beginning to congratulate myself. Siobhan, however, had taken in the entire episode and she was not terribly impressed.

"What a cop-out," she said.

Siobhan, let me note, is not given to subterfuge and guile. She is direct and candid to a fault. In a sense, her direct nature contrasts with her appearance. Have I mentioned that she is one of the natural beauties of the Western world? People have been moved to comment on her beauty since her time in a baby carriage and that year, at the age of thirteen, she had the kind of beauty that one associates with ballet dancers, that fine-featured, superdelicate quality that stops just short of fragility. Which is why it came as such a surprise to hear her talking on the phone one day and saying, "Oh, Don is such an asshole."

I couldn't believe my ears. It didn't seem possible that little Siobhan would say such a thing and I was stunned. How would Corinne handle this incident? Siobhan hung up the phone then and without so much as an apologetic glance in my direction, she stormed out after Liam who had done something entirely unforgiveable; he had taken her television chair while she was on the phone. "Oh, Liam," she said, "stop being such an asshole."

In a trice, I was beside her. Trying to control my own temper, I gave her the basic foul-speech-is-an-indication-of-ignorance speech. I told her it was particularly shocking to hear such a beautiful little girl use the kind of language that wouldn't be tolerated at the pool hall.

"I'm sorry," she said. "You're right."

For once, she was properly apologetic. She even went a step further and offered to make amends by shoveling the fresh fallen snow off the driveway. Although I agreed at once, Siobhan went off with her sled and the snow lay there untouched for the rest of the day. Later in the day I dispatched Liam to do the job but I was too hasty; what I failed to realize was that Siobhan *wanted* to shovel the snow, had been looking forward to it all day. When she walked up the cleared driveway, her sense of outrage grew. The reason I know this is the manner in which she greeted me: "Daddy, you're such an asshole."

It was open rebellion and should have been quashed then and there. But my main reaction was to burst into laughter.

"Your mother," I said, "will speak to you about that language when she comes home tonight."

Although the three children no longer believe in Santa Claus, they have retained a strong and devout belief in gifts. And, as I learned this year, while they don't believe in the Easter Bunny, they do believe in candy. During the week preceding Easter, there was much conjecture about how well I would handle my new assignment, the purchase of the candy eggs. I had to point out to the three of them that we were all too old to go through the charade of a giant bunny hippety-hopping in at night and depositing a basketful of potential dentist bills beside their beds.

"I'm not too old," eleven-year-old Liam said. "Are you trying to tell me there is *no* Easter Bunny?"

"Yeah, what're you trying to do," Sean said, "destroy a boy's faith?"

"Don't worry, Liam," Siobhan said. "There *is* an Easter Bunny. You'll see."

I was not about to give up without a struggle. As Easter came near, I clipped out newspaper stories reporting the rising cost of sugar and candy. I even located a story telling of a sudden, mysterious shortage of jelly beans. When the kids read the stories, they took action. They called every potential candy outlet in nearby villages and gave me the names of a dozen shops not yet hit by the mysterious jelly-bean shortage.

Corinne was the first to weaken. Responding to pressures she had felt each of the preceding fifteen years, she went into town and purchased large chocolate bunnies.

"I wanted them to have something," she said.

I did not sell out until late Saturday afternoon when I drove into town and picked up the jelly beans and the candy corn and the rest of it. Corinne had suggested I pick up Easter baskets for the candy, but in order to save six dollars, I thought of a rather ingenious way to avoid the purchase. This year we would use wooden salad bowls instead of baskets. Sure, why not?

Late that night, with the three children sound asleep, I carefully divided up the jelly beans, the chocolate, and the hard-boiled eggs and put the portions in wooden salad bowls. I knew the whole business was idiotic; still, there was a nice feeling to following the tradition; at least I had accomplished another motherly chore.

The next morning I awakened at nine o'clock and came out to find three rather glum children reading the Sunday papers.

"Well," I said, "did the Easter Bunny come?"

"*Some* Easter bunny," Sean said.

"What are you talking about?"

"There weren't even any baskets," Siobhan said. "Someone left the stuff in old salad bowls."

"But the candy must have been pretty good?" They went back to reading their papers without so much as a word of response. "What in the hell is going on here—you kids did get candy, right?"

148

"What there was of it," Sean said.

"There was plenty of candy there. Do you know what that stuff costs?"

"It took about five minutes to eat it," Siobhan said.

"I didn't take me that long," Liam said.

"You mean you ate all that stuff already? Your teeth are going to fall out of your heads. That does it—it is my sad duty to report, this year, the death of the Easter Bunny. Are you listening to me? There is no such thing as the Easter Bunny. Pay attention, Liam. There is no Easter Bunny."

"I can't hear you," Liam said.

I may have been a failure as an Easter Bunny, but I did somewhat better as a prophet; before the day was over, Liam did lose a tooth, one that had been loose for a week or so.

"Look at this tooth," he told me. "This is the biggest tooth I ever lost."

"To me, it's just another tooth," I said.

"Oh no," he said. "This is really a big one."

"Wonderful." I was still smarting over the candy.

"I think the good-tooth fairy will bring fifty cents for this one," he said.

"Liam, you are eleven years old and you should know by now there is no such thing as the good-tooth fairy. Also, for your future information, there is no such thing as Santa Claus. These are the harsh facts of life and you are old enough to face up to them."

"Never mind, Dad," he said. "It's not your job this year. I'll tell Mom about it."

Corinne is an old softy. When Liam explained to her that this was her year to be the good-tooth fairy, she seemed delighted.

"Do you have two quarters?" she asked me later in the night.

"You only need one."

"Liam said it was two."

"He's conning you—what would the good-tooth fairy know about inflation?"

"Oh, fifty cents is okay," she said. "It's my first time and I want to do it right."

A few moments later, she came back into the bedroom fifty cents poorer but smiling.

"Where's the tooth?" I said.

"What tooth?"

"Liam's tooth—the good-tooth fairy always brings back the tooth. Otherwise, the kid'll hit us for a second time tomorrow. It's under the pillow."

"Oh, *that's* where it is—I forgot where they were supposed to put it."

Neither of us made the transformation smoothly but we were each rewarded for the effort. The experiment did give me a close look at three kids who will be grown and gone before we know it. It was, in my eyes, the key reward. Often, to be sure, I found myself on unfamiliar terrain, wandering through a world that was new, but this, too, had its own set of rewards.

When Liam told me that I had to go to my first Teacher's Conference—"Mom always goes"—I was uncertain. I knew by this time that I should enter the world of the child with caution—taking care to avoid blunders that might embarrass him while attempting to be more than a mere sightseer.

The Teacher's Conference was scheduled for 2:10 P.M. of what had once been a working day. Of course, that is why it was a maternal ritual, one of those buzzingly dull routines that Corinne went through for years. Fifteen minutes before the appointed time, my car was in the school's parking lot. I watched the others as they arrived for their conferences—women in slacks and sweaters, one in jeans even, and I marveled at their insouciance. I had managed a haircut and two martinis before arriving too early.

Liam's directions from parking lot to classroom had been precise but incomplete. They made no mention of the distractions—the strange knee-level drinking fountains, the sudden alarm bells, the crayon drawings lining the corridors, all the nearly forgotten artifacts from my own past. The other parents—women all—were talking to the teachers inside the classroom. My son's teacher was still involved with another parent; clearly I was expected to sit on the folding chair left outside her door, sit down and wait, but I was too jumpy for that.

What would the teacher say to me? What judgment had she passed on my son? I marched the hallways restlessly, studying the crayoned leaves and witches and soldiers with an intensity one might accord so many Rembrandts. There were some of marked superiority—unsmudged, neatly drawn, symmetrical—but none of the drawings chosen for display bore the family name.

Of course not. Liam had doubtless inherited my all-thumbs approach to art. Oh, doubtless his teacher would want to get into that area, into all the inherited failings, into—who knows?—early evidence of moral disintegration and intellectual softness. How could I know about those things? Although I was becoming closer and closer to the kids, all I ever heard from Liam was of triumphs and conquests and glories, of A's on spelling tests, of bullies defeated, of home runs hit. And now this Teacher's Conference. Now the truth.

"You've been pacing out there," Mrs. Mailman said at the start of the conference.

"I get nervous whenever I'm in a school."

"Oh, I doubt that it was that bad an experience for you."

The teacher, Mrs. Mailman, was pleasant and attractive and friendly. I remembered the teachers from childhood as being older and larger, more matter-of-fact and level-of-head. But this teacher was different—she even seemed to have a sense of humor.

Before discussing Liam, she described the new approach to elementary-school teaching. The classrooms had been opened and the procedures were more flexible and the students were expected to develop their own sense of initiative. Initiative? I thought back, could remember Liam initiating softball games, trips to McDonald's, little else of substance. The teacher was explaining that small groups of children were banded together until specific intellectual problems were solved and then new groups were formed. I knew Liam as a player of games, a thrower of baseballs, a watcher of television—what would he know of these . . . specific intellectual problems?

The teacher wanted me to examine the boy's latest academic effort, a composition.

"It's over here," she said. "I couldn't put it in with the other papers because it would have stuck in the folder."

The reason it would have stuck in the folder was that it still bore the remains of what seemed to be several Oreo Creme Cookies. On the side of the composition there was also the clear imprint of what could only be the sole of a young boy's left sneaker.

Heart failing, I started to read.

151

"Monday led the week off to a good start. The week had flown by before I knew it." (Was that good? Bad? What do they expect from a mere boy?) "When I got to school Peggy asked me if I did my music. I said no." (What did they want, Hemingway?) "Boy, was Tony Lafala a pain to me."

All was saved, finally, when I came to the teacher's comments written in a contrastive, highly legible script: "Good job. This was written in an interesting manner."

So it wasn't going to be all bad. As I began to relax for the first time, Mrs. Mailman produced a mimeographed sheet, the Parent-Teacher Conference Form. And there was the summary of the boy's progress in school. It was all there. Social and Emotional Growth ("Enjoys participating in group activities") and Work Habits ("Works well independently") and Oral Language ("Speaks clearly and correctly") and Spelling ("Making good progress") and more.

The boy, then, was not doing badly at all. He was going to be all right. There was, of course, that one little clay-throwing incident. But what's a little clay thrown among friends? In a few minutes I was standing up, leaving.

"He's doing okay then?"

"Oh, you must be proud of him," she said.

Proud? The feeling went beyond pride. The feeling was one of relief.

TWENTY-FOUR

It was a fashionable summertime dinner party in New York. There were a movie critic and his wife, a stockbroker and his wife and two young men, both musicians, who shared the apartment across the hall from our host. The two young men made no effort to disguise the affection they felt for each other. We were seated with them at the dinner table and one of them, Jeff, asked me what I did for a living.

"Oh, I'm taking care of things around the house," I said. "I clean and cook and take care of the kids while Corinne is making the living this year."

"Is that so?" Jeff said, turning to Corinne. "And what do you do to make the living?"

"I manufacture and design things," she said.

"What kind of things?"

"You may have seen the cookbook stand," she said. "That's really been the mainstay of the business."

"The cookbook stand—no kidding," the second musician said. "Do you know that Jeff owns one of them? I don't think he could cook without it."

"No, I couldn't manage without it," Jeff said. "It's really one of the most marvelous things in my kitchen."

The conversation tended to make me uneasy. It was not that I found the young men annoying or even less than likable; it's just that the talk did make me uneasy. And after dinner, as Corinne stayed behind and carried on the conversation, I went into the living room and mingled with the other guests. Once the women found out that I had assumed the female role at home, and once they heard how hard I was finding it, they brought over their husbands to meet me and listen. I have been very popular with wives this year, not so popular with husbands.

When the two musicians finally came from the dining room, they behaved like any other old established married couple. They separated, went off to different conversations and every hour or so they got back together and touched bases. The one musician, Jeff, was spending most of his time in Corinne's company, a situation that couldn't have made me happier. And then it was two in the morning and I retrieved Corinne from the musician and started the long drive home.

"I'm so sorry you got stuck with that Jeff all night long," I said. "It couldn't have been much fun for you."

"Oh, he was very nice," she said. "I enjoyed our talk enormously."

"Did he ever discuss his homosexuality?"

"Not really," she said. "How did you know about that?"

"Who else would wear a floppy bow tie like that?"

"Wearing a bow tie does not automatically indicate homosex-

153

uality," Corinne said. "Another thing it might conceivably indicate is an awareness of fashion. Actually, he's not just a homosexual."

"What makes you say that?"

"Oh, there are ways to tell," she said.

"What ways?"

"For one thing, he used to be married."

"Doesn't mean a thing."

"Well, does it mean something if a man spends half the night propositioning you?"

"He did that?"

"He says he's bisexual."

I had overlooked that possibility altogether. This new bisexuality was going to be very confusing to old-fashioned people like myself, people who don't like their prejudices muddled up. All those hours I had been flirting with the other wives, all those hours I had been relaxing and enjoying myself, Corinne was being propositioned by a man ten years younger and, if the truth be known, considerably better-looking than her husband.

Hmmmm. As we drove home, I felt a hot flash of jealousy and then another. Early in our marriage we had agreed that jealousy was something we could do without and there have not been many moments given over to that particular emotion. But never before in the marriage had I been so vulnerable; never before had I relied on my mate for so many things. After a few months of not earning a living, one forgets that it is even possible to make a living. When I thought of having to pay the bills again, I imagined having to go back and start at the bottom again and slowly work my way up again. It was probably absurd, yet it was a possibility that could not be shaken.

Vulnerability was new to me, new and more than slightly bothersome. I've always been appreciative of Corinne's strengths, but now I was also beginning to see her as a meal ticket. She had become an excellent provider. And every time I heard the fact that the highest divorce rate in the country involved career women, I began to wonder why she would stay with me. Well, I could not afford to lose her to some young, good-looking musician with blond hair and a fashionably floppy bow tie. If she ever left me, I'd have to get a job.

154

Corinne had never been a deskbound executive. She spent at least a day or two every week out on the road—talking with salesmen, agents, factory owners, warehousemen and truckers. This year, of course, she was free to move around more than ever before.

The kids and I soon became accustomed to her coming home at unpredictable times. Sometimes she would be working at the office and just lose track of the time; other times she would be out on the road. Whenever she showed up late, I worried about the possibilities—accidents on the highway, smooth-talking salesmen in cozy bars. That last thought was such a cliché that I always succeeded in dismissing it almost immediately. I thought back to all those years when I called in late and I could appreciate what Corinne was going through. And that Friday near the end of the year when she showed up at ten, I tried not to let it bother me too much.

"Couldn't you have called?" I asked.

"I've been running all day," she said. "Believe me, there was just no way to . . ."

"You mean you were running all day and in all that running, you didn't see a single telephone?"

"The time I tried, the line was busy. I just didn't have enough time to sit around all day listening to busy signals. I'm famished. What's left from dinner?"

The hell with it. How many times had I come in after the appointed hour? And sometimes more than two or three hours late? Sometimes at four-thirty in the morning, when the last bar had closed and the first rays of the sun could be seen.

"Didn't you have time for lunch?" I asked.

"I did get a luncheon invitation, but I decided not to go."

"Who invited you?"

"Ace Drumbo," she said. "I told you about him. Mmmmm, this is still good. I sure married me a good cook."

"Told me what about Ace Drumbo?"

"I told you about him," she said. "He's the president of Drumbo plastics over in New Jersey. I guess he must have inherited the business from his father—he's still just a kid. What'd you put on the salad—whatever it is, it's perfect."

"How old is this kid?"

"Oh, I never can tell those things," she said. "You know, around thirty-five."

Ace Drumbo then, who was just a kid, was the same age as Corinne and only five years younger than myself. That made him the oldest kid in the neighborhood. Again I felt the presence of the green demon.

"What's this Ace Drumbo look like?"

"He's nowhere near as good-looking as you," Corinne sought to reassure me. "He's much too big. He looks like one of those professional football players. He must be six-foot-six. When he shakes hands with me, my hand just gets lost in his hand. Do you have any more chicken?"

"And he asked you out to lunch?"

"Yes, but I didn't have time."

"But you could have canceled your appointments," I said. "Why didn't you just go out with him?"

"Well, because it frankly didn't seem right," she said. "I mean, it was all proper and above-board—his secretary was going to go along with us—it's just that I asked myself a simple question; was there a genuine reason for us to have lunch together or would it have been more of a social event? By that time we had gotten most of our business done and I decided that it was just going to be social."

"Very good reasoning," I said.

"And I don't want to go out with any men for just social reasons."

"That's probably a good guideline," I said. "Ready for dessert now?"

There are times when I can be an unqualified phony. A few years before, when I was editing a weekend newspaper supplement, I had been given an expense account and the encouragement to uncover new talent. Well, I invited many promising young male writers to my office for conferences and I had similar conferences with young female writers, similar except that often they took place at a small Italian restaurant in a nearby town. If I had employed Corinne's guidelines, I would have had a livelier magazine and a duller lunch hour.

"This Ace Drumbo," I said, "is he married?"

I was trying not to seem too interested. But jealousy was a fairly new emotion and I was not yet certain how to express it properly.

"Oh yes, he's married," Corinne said. "He has pictures of his kids all over the office—five of them."

"Pictures of his wife?"

"No, I don't think so."

"Those are the worst kind," I said.

"What do you mean? Worst kind of what?"

"Those so-called family men," I heard myself saying. "Pictures of the kids and none of the wife and asking other broads out to lunch. I mean, does he even realize that you're married?"

"It never came up."

Never came up? What was that supposed to mean? The little green demon jumped on my back and stuck it to me hard. *Never came up?* As I said, there are times when I can certainly be an out-and-out phony. How many times did I go out of my way to establish that I was married when some female was batting her eyes in my direction? Neither Corinne nor I wore wedding bands. Years before, when we had gotten married, I had decided that wearing a ring was slightly unmanly and Corinne had decided, fine, she wouldn't wear a ring either. That night, for the first time, I was beginning to think it might not be such a bad idea if we both started wearing wedding rings.

"This Ace Drumbo sounds pretty suspicious to me," I said. "Another Vincent. I wonder what *his* wife would say if she knew he was inviting women out to lunch."

"She wouldn't mind in the least."

"How can you say that?"

"It's easy," Corinne said. "The reason I know she wouldn't mind is that she was there; she's his secretary. Can I have my dessert now?"

TWENTY-FIVE

It took the better part of a year, but it finally happened; I began to miss the glamour of the old life. In all that time I had not lunched out more than once or twice. The credit cards were slipping farther and farther back into my wallet. I had once worked in an office filled with pretty secretaries, and I hadn't seen one of that species in all my time at home. There were times when life seemed to be painted in overlapping shades of gray.

When an old friend, Larry Smith, called to suggest a lunch, I was in no mood to refuse. I showed up at his office at noon, punctually. Larry's success as an architect was evidenced everywhere in his new suite of offices. Floor-to-ceiling tinted windows looking out over the Long Island landscape, everything glass and chrome and leather. And, sitting behind a desk seemingly designed to reveal the full length of her legs, there was a young woman who must have been all of nineteen years old.

"Good afternoon, Mr. McGrady," she said.

"How did you know?"

"Mr. Smith just called from Long Beach," she said. "The traffic is just terrible and he said that I'm supposed to make you feel comfortable while you're waiting. So, if you'll just follow me, please."

I still slip so easily into traditional male attitudes. I knew better but even as I was following her, I allowed her miniskirt to distract me. I might as well admit it; some things are beyond my grasp. I know how a liberated human being should react; I know how someone with a properly raised consciousness would react; but what I was thinking was that it was certainly remarkable how long and pretty her legs were.

"Now you sit right here and make yourself at home," she said, "while I get you some coffee."

"Black, please."

As she went for the coffee, I finally managed to examine my surroundings. The paintings were modern, as were the furnishings. Huge windows opened up the space, and soft music came from a stereo set in the corner. The receptionist returned with the coffee and even went to the trouble of stirring in the sugar for me.

"Now is there anything else?" she said. "Mr. Smith said I was to make you *very* comfortable."

"Well, you've certainly done that."

Which was not quite the truth. In point of fact, she had been making me very nervous. As she left, I once again marveled at the length of leg emerging from that shortness of skirt. No sooner had she gone, than a second young woman appeared. If anything, she seemed prettier than the first one. I must say, Larry had a well-run office. The new arrival, doubtless acting on instructions, offered me a guided tour of the offices and concluded it just as Larry walked into the room.

"How about a little something?" Larry said. "Still drinking Jack Daniel's?"

"Just to be sociable," I said.

I hadn't noticed the bar in the corner. Until he opened it, it looked like a small desk. After pouring with his customary heavy hand, Larry cleared up a few business matters. There were some last-minute instructions to beautiful girl number one and beautiful girl number two, and then some final phone calls. I listened as he said, "Well, if you can't do it that way—if you can't use the proper materials—then let's not bother to do it at all." The reason the details stay in mind is that they were all so far removed from my life.

This process continued as we drove to Larry's favorite restaurant, where he was greeted like a long-lost son. The owner came out and then the chef. Did Larry want his steak done the usual way? And, instead of the french fries, did he want some of Mama's special cannelloni? And how was the family?

It brought back memories, not too distant memories. The low rumble of conversation set against the bell tones of female laughter, the glitter of silver and glass and ice, it all brought back memories of my old favorite restaurant. But that was another life. We ordered another round, and back home there was laundry to do and floors to be waxed and kids about to come home from school, but all of that was distant, unreal.

In the manner of businessmen with no time to waste on the niceties, we had our lunches brought to the bar. At a table not a dozen steps away were two women having lunch. The women were perhaps ten years younger than Larry or myself. One of the women was looking directly at me, staring actually. I must admit that this phenomenon didn't stir any old memories.

"Larry, you tell me, is that girl looking at me?"

"I believe she is," he said.

Had I become that attractive in less than a year? Hmmm, that was an intriguing possibility. I ignored the stare and looked the other way but it was one of those stares that it was difficult to ignore. Nor was it sufficient to just turn my back on her. A moment later she came up to the bar, stood less than six feet away, continued to stare. Finally she said something.

"Okay, where do I know you from?"

"Me?"

"Yes, I know you," she said, "but where from?"

"This is Mike McGrady," Larry said. "Maybe you used to read his column."

"Oh, that explains it," she said. "Yes, I read your column."

Her answer indicated that she was probably a political conservative. Conservatives, the ones who said anything at all, had always said they read the column. Liberals, on the other hand, would say they liked the column. There's a considerable difference. Other than being a probable conservative, she was a definite honey blonde with a slight scattering of freckles across a pug nose. Even after learning my identity, she was still staring. When I turned around this time, she gave me a smile that would light up any barroom.

I had had a half-dozen bourbons by this time and was having some difficulty making out the letters of a golden pendant she was wearing on her blouse. When she noticed my interest, she came over and held it so that I could read the lettering while, at the same time, making it easier for me to examine the surface the pendant was resting on. The lettering spelled out this: "I'm Good."

"I suppose that's a good thing to establish right away," I said.

"Oh, you must be reading it incorrectly," she said. It doesn't say, 'I'm good.' It says, 'I'm *Goooooooooooood!'*"

"Good but not great?"

"I think that depends entirely upon my partner," she said, giving me another one of those smiles. What was happening to me? First in Larry's office and now in the restaurant, I was finding myself closely studying members of the opposite sex. This one said her name was Marti.

"What do you do?" I asked.

"Oh, just about anything I can get away with," she said.

"No, seriously," I said. "What do you do with your days? Are you married? Do you have children?"

"What boring questions," she said. "I'll tell you this much—

160

what I do with my days is nowhere near as interesting as what I do with my nights."

Why was I sitting there listening to this kind of stuff? Marti was all too obviously a veteran of the singles-bar wars and there was no way for me to carry on a coherent conversation with her. I went back to the dinner. When the coffee arrived, both women—Marti and her often-married older sister—joined us. Getting solid information about them proved next to impossible, since they bantered instead of talked. However, it finally emerged that they were both married, both mothers, both bored, and both killing an afternoon in the manner they liked best, flirting.

"What a way to spend a day," I said.

"Don't knock it," Marti said. "And besides, look at yourself—you're here just as much as we're here." At this point she turned to Larry. "You know something, your friend's starting to make me nervous. Besides, you're much cuter."

Larry seemed not to hear. Showing himself to be a man of impeccable taste, he turned his back on the two women and resumed our conversation until they finally vanished. At midafternoon Larry had to return to the office and it was time for me to go back home; he left but I didn't. Soon the late-afternoon shift arrived, the local businessmen knocking off work a couple of hours early, and housewives, arriving in pairs, sitting at the bar, comparing giggles, allowing the nearest time-killing executive to sign his name to their bar tabs. One hour reached out for another and I found myself involved in lengthy, weighty conversations regarding the respective merits of songs on the jukebox, of cars on the road. Gradually, all the responsibilities of home vanished.

Home. I didn't want a repeat of my afternoon in the topless bar several months earlier. Fortunately, this time the answering female voice belonged to my daughter, not my wife. I told Siobhan that Daddy was giving the family a little treat tonight; she was to tell Mommy that she had to take the family out to McDonald's, because Daddy had been held up with Uncle Larry on important business matters.

"Neato!" Siobhan said.

I went back to the bar. The other males at the bar were tanned and were speaking about their recent vacations to Caracas or to the islands. They talked about profits turned in real estate deals. The conversations, peppered with such words as "windfall" and "bonanza," were all pitched just loud enough so that nearby females could hear. The women listened in and accepted the drinks, and there was an occasional rub of hip against hip and shoulder against shoulder. If it went beyond that, I didn't notice.

The next time I consulted a clock, it was midnight. The barmaid had changed faces and several new shifts of drinkers had come and gone. I had gotten into dozens of pointless conversations, eavesdropped on others, and still I was reluctant to go home. It was one of two or three inexplicably late nights the entire year, but it made me face up to the situation. There was no reason for my being there. Well, only one. There comes a time when the house is a cage and the family seems to be a warden, a time when the sheer glamourlessness of it all finally gets to you, a time when you find yourself face to face with your own loneliness.

TWENTY-SIX

"You never take me out any more," I was saying to Corinne one night in September. "When we were courting, it was a different story. A new restaurant every night. All the best shows . . ."

"As a matter of fact," she said, "we have been invited out to dinner, but I already said no. I still can't get used to the fact that you're willing to go out."

"Why don't you call them back?" I said.

The invitation had come from Roger and Sally, next-door neighbors from another time and another neighborhood. We were joined by Jack and Maureen, two people we had never met. That night during dinner the discussion quickly got around to the subject of women's liberation. When Corinne announced that I was in charge of the housewifely tasks this year, there were the usual double-takes followed by the usual moment of stunned silence.

More than two lives had been affected by our swap. Corinne and I, of course, had the most adjusting to do. But I never anticipated that the changeover would also affect the lives of others—relatives, friends, and even strangers.

"You're doing *everything* around the house?" Maureen said. "I can't believe that."

"Why not?" her husband, Jack, asked. "There's not really that much to do."

"I enjoy doing things around the house," Roger said.

As it turned out, Roger, a prominent lawyer, had spent the afternoon making our dessert. Chocolate mousse. The hard way. Not only had he missed most of the televised football game, he had thoroughly enjoyed the experience.

"But it doesn't seem to me you have to totally reverse roles," Sally said. "Roger enjoys doing some things around the house and, fine, those are the things he should do."

"You won't get any argument from me," Roger said.

"No, I want to go farther with this," Sally said. "It's almost as though you and Corinne feel a woman can't find herself within the confines of marriage. Some can't—but some can. I think I'm one of those people who can. Take my mother, for example; she was always the strongest part of the family. Dad made the money and paid the bills, but that had nothing to do with it—he seemed colorless beside her. He worked twelve–fourteen hours a day as a foreman in a textile plant. Big deal. Mother ran the household—but really *ran* it, you know—and when things got tight, she didn't think twice, she went out and worked. She had all the strength in the world."

Jack and Maureen were not participating in the discussion. They seemed content to take it all in. At the end of the meal, we moved into the living room for the coffee and the dessert. Roger's efforts had been rewarded by a superb mousse.

"This is terrific," I said. "I've tried it a couple of times but this is the best I've had."

"Why don't you ask Roger for his recipe," Jack said. "I'm sure he'll give it to you."

"It *is* delicious," Maureen agreed, "but I never thought I'd see the day when Roger would be happy puttering about the kitchen."

"Roger will make someone a lovely wife," Jack chimed in.

"Except for one little thing," Sally said, joining the attack.

"Everytime Roger goes near the kitchen, it takes me four hours to clean up the pots. Tonight, I must admit, the results are worth it."

"Yes, Roger," Jack said, "you *must* give us your recipe."

Jack wouldn't let up. A middle-aged businessman of obvious affluence, he had inherited the family business and married Maureen, his former secretary, three years earlier. They had no children of their own, but she was raising his four children by an earlier marriage.

"I've been thinking over all this talk," Jack said, "and I don't see why you people make such a big deal out of role reversal. What you're doing is not all that unusual. I don't think you'll find many men these days who would come home from work and park themselves in front of the television set and expect to be waited on hand and foot."

"No?" Maureen asked the question.

"Absolutely not!" Jack seemed just the slightest bit angry. "Most men work fourteen or fifteen hours a day trying to get their business started, or trying to get their business going, and whatever pampering they get at home, well, they deserve it."

"Well, which is it?" Maureen said.

"Which is what?"

"Do most men come home and pitch in without being pampered? Or do most men come home and get the kind of pampering they so richly deserve?"

"It should work both ways," Jack said. "I don't think our case is all that unusual. You take pretty damn good care of me and we divide the household duties right down the middle."

"Right down the middle, ninety-ten," she said.

"What's that supposed to mean?"

"That's supposed to mean we don't divide any of the real work," Maureen said. "You don't expect to have dinner on the table—and hot—the minute you walk in the door? You don't expect me to make the beds every morning?"

"Well, whatever pampering I do get," Jack said, "is not entirely undeserved, if you know what I mean. I make a good living, a pretty damn good living, and you and the kids don't have to do without anything."

"We're not arguing about that."

164

"Well, dammit, that's the crux of the matter." I could feel the conversation taking a brutish turn. "Corinne here happens to be paying the bills. I don't know how many of our bills you think you could pay on a secretary's salary. But maybe if you were, maybe if you started to pay all the bills, we could talk about my making the beds."

"You have to admit, it's not the easiest thing in the world, trying to make the money to pay bills when I have to pick up after you and the four kids. . ."

"Maureen!"

The single word of warning sufficed. Both Maureen and Jack realized they had gone too far in front of strangers, and there was a moment of silence before we tried to steer the conversation back onto safer ground.

It was such a common reaction this year that I was no longer surprised. The prospect of role reversal is threatening to almost everyone. When we have finally solved the problems attached to being a man or a woman, when we have repeated the solutions over and over again, when we have finally become comfortable with them, it is not easy to contemplate abandoning all we have learned for a brand-new set of problems. Maureen, who had been attacking her husband for not helping around the house, quickly began attacking Roger for having done just that.

"Yes," she said. "I've heard that Roger is thinking of going to Denmark for a little operation."

"Oh," Sally said, "did I tell you about the mess he made in the kitchen? Eleven different pots and bowls, *eleven* pots and bowls to make that little mousse we just ate. I swear, I hope Roger never tries to surprise me with breakfast in bed again. Those mornings I hate to get out of bed because I know what's going to be waiting for me out there in the kitchen. It looks like Hiroshima."

"You know what, honey?" Roger said. "As a matter of fact, I think you did mention that earlier."

The women's reactions constantly surprised me. I could anticipate the male reactions; I could guess that they would not be anxious to give up their freedom for the pleasures of housework. What startled me this year was the reaction of Maureen and Sally. I would never have guessed that they would be so threatened by the loss of servant's status. Roger had managed a faultless chocolate mousse, and no one in the room seemed able to accept that fact.

Well, the fact is this: it is perfectly possible for a person of either sex to walk into a kitchen and make an acceptable meal. But, for reasons of their own, many women don't want this information broadcast too widely. Perhaps this is because most women don't realize it would be just as easy for them to walk into the business offices of the world and, with suitable training, run an office or manage a team of salesmen or do whatever mysterious thing their husbands do all day long.

Roles *are* reversible. There is some risk involved, but there are also compensations, rewards that make the risks seem insignificant. Most of us are not gamblers; most of us would prefer to stick with doing the things we have always done, with solving the problems we have already solved. And as this particular evening came to an end, as everyone retreated back into their old, comfortable roles, I could feel the relief.

If our little experiment has sometimes been a strain on friends, it has been an even greater ordeal on close relatives.

I have always gotten along famously with my wife's parents. Corinne's father, Albert Young, the former president of five chemical companies, has lived the life of a modern-day Horatio Alger. He came up from the streets of Brooklyn to a six-acre estate in Sands Point. Today, he and Reda, an accomplished artist, live in a small palace bordering a Florida golf course. Their achievements did not come easily. Even during the last years of his working life, he rose at six every morning and battled the rush-hour traffic to his factory where he routinely put in twelve-hour days. They both found the good life; but they found it through hard work and creative imagination.

And now they found themselves with a son-in-law who quit his well-paying job so that he might spend his days cooking and cleaning.

I had put them through similar trials in the past and their affection had survived. Whenever we had gotten a little ahead of the game, I had found an excuse to take a leave of absence. One time we packed the kids in a camper and traveled throughout the country. Another time I had just learned the game of golf and didn't want to stop playing. They had, at any rate, through the years gotten accustomed to the sight of their son-in-law not working.

Every summer the Youngs come north and spend three months on Long Island. During those summer months we will get together at least once a week. Most often, they come to the house, check the growth rate of their grandchildren, and have dinner with us. Their first visit they could hardly help but notice that their daughter was sitting with them, discussing the affairs of the world, while her husband was bustling around in the kitchen wearing an apron. Before too long, I was joined by Albert.

"Tell me this, Mike," he said, "when are you going to go back to work?"

"Gee, I . . ."

"Everyone misses your column," he said, "and that's a fact. Everyone I talk to wishes you were back working with the paper."

There were—that first night and throughout the summer—repeated inquiries about my future plans, my job prospects, my long-range ambitions. But never did either Albert or Reda reveal any impatience with their slightly peculiar son-in-law. Well, there *was* that one night in late August.

We had been sitting outside that evening, and, as always, both Youngs had been effusive in their praise of my cooking. I must concede that the dinner had turned out well. Barbecued steak, potatoes Anna, a variety of fruits and vegetables. We sat around afterward, enjoying the cool of twilight, waiting for the mosquitoes to begin their nightly assault, and Albert patted his stomach in appreciation.

"Well, now I know what I'm going to get you next Christmas," he said.

"What's that, Dad?"

"Next Christmas," he said, "I'm going to buy you a nice housecoat."

My own parents took the switch somewhat more seriously. Not without reason. They had three children, all boys, and they had seen two of them through Yale and one through Harvard. The other two had given up regular employment for the perils of freelancing much earlier. When I, too, stopped receiving a pay check,

167

it meant that they had parented one of the most overeducated, underemployed families around. Understandably then, when they were told of the decision, there were some serious discussions. Generally, they took this form: "I only hope you know what you're doing." Or this form: "It's *your* life." Or this form: "Are you sure you don't want to reconsider?"

A family that was out of work—and looking—during part of the Great Depression cannot easily accept a son giving up a first-rate job to become a housewife. Similarly, a family that has always cast the male as breadwinner doesn't quite believe that a woman can pay all the bills.

Before too long, however, they accepted both propositions. And about the same time my mother became a treasury of small encouragements.

Should we visit them in their city apartment, my mother would produce a letter from a grandson on the West Coast: "He says he's learning how to cook. He's already made some entire dinners. It's so good for a boy to learn how to cook these days. And, believe me, there's nothing sissy about it."

And later she would say: "You know something, it's just amazing how many of the great chefs in the world are men. I read that the other day. Almost all of them, with just one or two exceptions, are men. Real men, too. There's nothing sissy about knowing how to cook."

And still later: "Oh, by the way, I cut a story from the newspaper the other day, this'll interest you. It says that many of the great universities are teaching cooking classes now. Not just home economics—but real cooking classes. And you know something—let me find it here, yes—at least as many men as women are taking the courses."

And then my father would say, "Jeez, Mike, what're you going to do when you go back to work? I mean, have you got any idea yet where you're going to look for a job?"

As the year went on, the family attitudes continued to soften. Even my father, who, let me note parenthetically, is the son of a copper miner and the toughest man ever to grace the uniform of the United States Marine Corps, took great pains to tell me that he, too, was learning how to cook. When my mother had to leave for several weeks to help out an ailing sister, he decided to do his

168

own cooking. I was very impressed by this until I overheard him asking Corinne a culinary question.

"You know those little jars of cocktail frankfurters?" he said. "You can practically live on those things. There's just one thing I haven't figured out yet—what's the best way to cook them?"

Late in the year, my mother came out to visit us for a few days and I sensed that she was enthusiastically accepting the idea now. She was watching my every move around the kitchen with obvious motherly pride and on two separate occasions I saw her eyes actually light up.

That first morning, as she was starting on her coffee, I began assembling a chicken-tarragon omelet. It wasn't that, the omelet, that lit up her eyes. But when she saw me take all the chicken bones, dump them in a pot of boiling water, add some carrots, onions, and turnips, getting a soup started for the next day's use, that's when I saw the glow in her eyes.

The other time this phenomenon was observed came later that day when she was talking to Corinne.

"Yes, the business is growing almost too large," Corinne was saying. "In fact, I've got to get additional office space. What I'm really looking for is an office with warehouse space attached. But there's nothing like that available in Northport."

"Well, surely you could find something like that over in Huntington," my mother said.

"To tell you the truth," Corinne said, "I wouldn't feel right being that far away from the kids and the home."

That was the second time her eyes lit up.

Family members went from skepticism to questioning to acceptance within the space of a year. It helped when they realized that the meals were going to be cooked and the bills were going to be paid, and while the whole thing was a little peculiar, everyone was going to survive our idiosyncrasies.

I didn't tell everyone about my new life as a housewife. For example, I spared the regular drinkers at the Pier Three all the details. Of course, most of them hadn't yet come to terms with the old tradition, the one where the husband pays the bills, and I was sure my current situation would prove confusing. As it turned out, I didn't have to be all that reticent.

Linda, the barmaid, had long had a weakness for mayonnaise. Through the long afternoons, surrounded by grizzled old men attempting to remain upright, she would take slices of fresh tomato and dip them into a small bottle of mayonnaise and eat them.

"You know," I told her one day, "you really ought to make your own mayonnaise. There's nothing to it."

"Are you kidding? I can't boil water."

"You don't even have to boil water," I said. "Look, I'll bring you in some of mine."

"*Yours?* You mean your wife's."

"No, mine." I lowered my voice. "I'm doing all the cooking this year. I'll bring you some tomorrow. You'll see."

"I won't hold my breath."

"You'll see."

"Sure I will."

So young and so skeptical. Well, Linda had listened to many offers in her time, the full line of propositions, but this was the first time a male ever offered to bring her mayonnaise. The next day at noon I did bring her a small jar of freshly made mayonnaise and was rewarded by an expression of suprise that came close to out-and-out shock. And this was replaced, as she tasted it, by an expression bordering on the beatific.

"Would you marry me?" she said, then turned to speak to the regulars at the bar. "Hey, everyone, you've got to try this mayonnaise. Mike made it himself."

"What're you tryna tell us?" a white-haired man asked. "Are you tryna tell us you can make mayonnaise at home?"

"Sure, there's nothing to it."

The mayonnaise was well received. Before the afternoon was out, I had to write the recipe on a half-dozen cocktail napkins. I don't know whether anyone there that afternoon ever actually went to the trouble of making mayonnaise. But I do know this: at that moment, with a bunch of unshaven men asking me for my recipe for mayonnaise, I stopped worrying about what the rest of the world was going to think of my new role in life.

TWENTY-SEVEN

It strikes me that I've been unfair. I've presented too bleak a portrait of the housewifely existence. There have been compensations, rewards, moments I wouldn't have traded with anyone.

This year, when the upperclassmen of the Norwood Avenue elementary school made their annual trip to the nation's capital, Liam went along. He was the third and final McGrady youngster to make the trip. In a sense, it was more than a visit to Washington; it was also three days away from home and family, a passage into apprentice adulthood.

The only unpleasant aspect of the trip was its time of departure. Four o'clock in the morning. And, as so often during the year, I was once again a solitary male figure in a female world. It is important that the breadwinner face the new day with a full night's sleep, that the provider be provided with a well-rested psyche, and so the chauffeurs that early morning were the mothers and myself.

"You going to eat all your food down there?" I asked Liam.

"Sure," he said.

"What if you don't like it?"

"Well, I made five sandwiches just in case," he said. "Peanut butter. I've got them in the suitcase."

"Peanut butter? Inside the suitcase?"

"Don't worry about them," he said. "I wrapped them up in the shirts."

"Liam . . ."

"Just kidding, Dad."

My son got out of the car then and joined the procession toward the chartered bus. There he was, neighborhood tough guy, wearing new trousers, blue blazer, and a necktie we had chopped down from one of my old models that very morning. Liam McGrady, carrying camera and overnight bag and maybe some peanut-butter sandwiches, openly enthusiastic about his debut in the outside world.

As I watched him climb up onto that airport bus with his fellow sixth-graders, there was a lump in my throat that couldn't be swallowed. I had missed this moment with the other two children. Through the years I had missed quite a bit by being no more than a father.

By the time I was back home, it was too late to grab a few winks and too early to awaken the others. I sat drinking coffee and rereading old newspapers until Corinne appeared. She was in a rush and she drank at a cup of coffee on her way toward the door.

"Oh, dear, would you take these books to the library for me?" she said. "There's one with a dollar fine—that's Liam's book on airplanes—if you don't have enough to pay for it, stop by the office. Another thing, we're low on vitamin C and while you're at the health-food store, you might want to get some safflower oil . . ."

"Well . . ."

"Another thing." She was at the door now. "Would you drive over to the apple farm and pick up some apples. And while you're there, you may as well get some cider."

"I'm not sure I'll have the time . . ."

"Well, if you have the time . . ."

The door was closing behind her but she was still talking, remembering another possible errand. No sooner was the door closed than Siobhan came out of the bathroom.

"Did you make lunch yet?" she asked.

"Yes."

"Oh God."

"What's the matter now?"

"I wanted to tell you not to use the Russian dressing on the sandwiches."

"But that's homemade Russian dressing—you liked it fine last night when it was on the salad."

"Yeah, it's okay on salad," she said, "but it's terrible on sandwiches."

"Suffer!"

By this time, Sean was staggering around in his bathrobe, blinking away the sleep from his eyes, going through his usual early-morning struggle to determine where he was and who these people were who were living with him. Gradually, it all came back to him.

"It's bowling day today," he said.

172

"Have a good game."

"Yeah, I'll call you when I miss my bus."

"You mean *if* you miss your bus."

"I always miss my bus," he said. "So I'll call you when I miss my bus."

And then finally they were all gone. The year before I would have slept through Liam's departure, would have been the one running out of the house with a coffee cup in my hand. This year I was part of everyone else's life. True, I was the servant, the deliveryman, the cook, and the chauffeur—but at least I was part of their lives. Let them put the knock on my Russian dressing; let them order me around; at least they were using me. At the end of the year they had all accepted me in the role and that was not a bad feeling. So don't let me neglect to mention some of the joys of motherhood, even this belated and male motherhood of mine.

Some days I was more content in the role than others. On this day I went off to run my errands with a full heart. I stopped at the health-food store for the safflower oil and the vitamins, and I found that the shop was being run by a young woman who had once been our baby sitter. Since last I had seen her, Daisy had acquired a husband, two children, and now a thriving business.

"We're following opposite courses," I said to her "I've given up my job to stay home and you're giving up motherhood to stay in business."

"You're the smart one," Daisy said.

"That's the first time anyone has said that. Usually people look at me as though I've lost a marble or two."

"You're not crazy," she said. "I'm the one who's crazy. Look at me. What am I doing this for? I had it made."

"But you're making a living."

"You know what that means," she said. "All that means is that we can afford to pay the bills a little sooner than we used to. But the headaches! I'm telling you, the way this food spoils, sometimes I'm tempted to add a few preservatives. Not that I would, Mr. McGrady. But here I am, on my feet all day long, and I don't even know my family anymore. Let me tell you, I could give you the reverse side of women's liberation."

"Today you're speaking to the right person," I said. "Today I know what you're talking about."

"Just yesterday my little boy got a nail in the eye," she said. "Right near his eye and there was no one around who could take him to the doctor. What am I doing here when something like that can happen? And you should see the dinners we eat some nights. A year ago I wouldn't give food like that to a dog. And I hate dogs."

Another voice heard from, and one I could not be deaf to. I found many aspects of the housewife's life pleasurable, chief among these the absence of pressure. It took some time to get used to the notion that I didn't have to make money, but once that realization settled in, it was as if an enormous weight had been lifted from my shoulders. Unfortunately, it was not that the weight had disappeared; it had just settled on a different set of shoulders.

As the year progressed, Corinne's hours became longer and longer. Although she claimed to enjoy paying the bills, she was learning exactly what it costs to support a family. And what it cost was what she was making. Despite the faltering national economy, her business doubled in volume and her personal income had gone from roughly $10,000 a year to roughly $20,000. However, maintaining the family came to just over $20,000 and she was, at year's end, slightly poorer than when it began. But poorer only in a limited sense.

"I think something more important than my income has changed," she said one night. "My attitudes have changed toward many things. I can deal with authority now. I couldn't before."

It took Corinne time to adjust completely to her new responsibilities. For several months, she ran the business as she always had, spending long days typing out shipping labels, doing the billing, writing the dunning letters. But as she learned that her time was money, the old ways of running a business no longer sufficed. In September, just as I was feeling free enough to go out and shoot a round of golf every now and then, she was feeling free enough to hire her first employee, an office assistant who could come in and do the clerical work several hours a day.

Still, business pressures took a toll. More and more often, Corinne would arrive home at night too weary to even try to fake happiness. If she happened to come home early, before the dinner was on the table, she would retreat into the living room and hide her mood behind an evening newspaper.

174

In November, with the pre-Christmas pressures mounting, Corinne clearly needed a break. I suggested that she get away for a few days, and this time she didn't hesitate; she headed for Boston with her friend Stella.

While she was away, I took the business messages and tallied up the checks for her. And at night, when she called, I passed along only the good news. The Boston trip was a milestone of sorts, the first time Corinne ever felt it necessary to escape business pressures. If she had been in business all of her life, perhaps she would understand the therapeutic value of a round of golf or the medicinal justification of two martinis before supper. What she did was explore a city she had always loved, do the kind of shopping she hadn't found time for in months, dine out at good restaurants, and, in brief, escape.

Just listening to her suddenly cheerful voice on the phone was enough to cheer me up. In a way, it was a vacation for me as well. For the first time in many months, I wasn't subjected to the same business worries she was feeling. Her absence was reflected on the dinner table; those lovingly home-cooked meals we had been having for months vanished with Corinne. The first night I served frankfurters. The second night, pizza. The third night, after Sean asked when Mom was coming home, guilt overcame me and I served a roast chicken. And finally Corinne came home, rested and relaxed, and she made the mistake of opening her mail.

Incidentally, almost all of the mail was her mail. Over the past year, as far as the postman was concerned, I had become an invisible man. We were receiving at least a dozen pieces of mail a day, and only one or two of those envelopes were addressed to me. As a result, Corinne had taken to letting me have all those correspondences addressed to "Homeowner" or "Occupant." It was just as well. Corinne's mail was not all checks. It was bills; it was a report that the United Parcel strike was continuing; it was a collection of breakage reports; it was a letter of complaint about her new plastic polish.

And then Corinne came to the most important piece of mail, her new catalogue, a project that she had spent several weeks supervising. Corinne was ready to mail out thousands of the catalogues, a mailing that would open up a brand-new side to her business. However, through a printer's miscalculation, all of the photographed items were pictured against a murky background; it was impossible to determine whether they were constructed of clear plastic or, oh, mahogany.

"I can't believe it!" A shriek. "I can't believe anyone would do anything this dumb!"

"Take it easy," I said, striving for a soothing tone. "It'll be all right."

"All right?" Well, maybe not. "I don't understand how anyone stays in business. Anyone. For me to get anything done properly, and I mean anything at all, I've got to do it myself. Over these past four months I've done everything myself. I go away for just a few days and someone makes a wrong decision, the only possible wrong decision, and the whole project goes down the drain."

"Can't this wait until tomorrow?"

"The trouble is it has to wait until tomorrow."

"Good, why don't we just forget it until then?" I said. "Why don't we go to bed and get a good night's sleep. Tomorrow morning you can call the printers and get things going again."

"Tomorrow is too late," she said. "Today is too late. There is no possible way these pictures can be corrected in time for me to mail them out. I'm telling you, I wish I had never come home."

"You don't mean that."

"I'm so tired of this. I'm so tired of not being able to trust another person in the whole world."

"These pictures aren't that bad," I said. "People will be able to figure out they're made of plastic . . ."

"They're not supposed to have to figure anything out," she said. "That's the reason I have photographs. So people won't have to figure out anything for themselves."

"Since there's nothing we can do about it, why don't we just relax?"

"What you don't understand"—whenever Corinne uses that phrase, the discussion is over—"what you can't possibly know, is a thing like this can put me right out of business. You don't have any idea how serious this can be."

"I'm beginning to have some idea."

"Sometimes I would like to chuck this whole business," she said. "I would really like to find something I enjoy doing. I don't

176

know why I've got to go on putting up with this kind of thing . . ."

"I've got an idea," I said. "Why don't you stay home this next year and be the housewife? I'll pay all the bills."

"Let's go to bed," she said.

It was November and the trade had been for a year, only a year. I knew we should be asking ourselves what we were going to do next, but every time the subject came up, Corinne put off the decisions. It was as if we could avoid the decision by simply ignoring the passage of time.

In point of fact, the year had gone by quickly, and at the end of it, I was just becoming accustomed to some aspects of the housewife's life.

In many ways, it had not been a true test for me. Despite what you may have read here, there was a broad variety of factors in conspiracy to make the year as pleasant as possible for me.

Any woman saddled with infants will know just how easy I had it. When babies are still in diapers, there is no simple escape, no way to slip off to the pool hall or the tavern for a break in routine. Whenever someone did visit us with toddlers, my frustration quotient jumped sizably. If I had had the problem of a baby, in addition to the problems I faced, I might not have endured the year.

Then, too, money was never the problem it might have been. Had we tried the same trade a few years earlier, back before Corinne's business was well launched, it would have been much more challenging. The main challenge would have been remaining alive without food or money; by my calculations, our money would have run out about midway through the third week of August.

Another key mitigating factor, one that I always kept in mind, was the temporary nature of the switch. It was for a year, no more. No one tells a new bride that she is only going to be a housewife for a year. The difference between a year in prison and a life sentence is considerable.

The year had been boring, repetitive, dreary, and at times just dumb—yet, I had enjoyed it more than any year in recent memory. At least I had been aware of it. In living a life of deadlines, a

177

life where one assignment overlaps another, time vanishes. This year I took walks and noted season changes and enjoyed sunsets.

This year I became a real part of the family, maybe for the first time. This year it was I who had to make the small decisions and help with the homework and nag about the unmade beds—and, at the same time, spend more hours playing more games than any time since my own boyhood.

I'm in better shape physically than at any time during the past ten years. A December physical examination showed blood pressure down near normal, weight down twenty pounds, all other medical indicators up.

The realization that the year was coming to an end came as a surprise. The future was cloudy. In December I didn't know whether I should start looking for a job and, if so, what kind of a job. All I felt for sure was that my days as a housewife were coming to an end. I had enjoyed much of it, had hated some of it, but was anxious to be done with it. I suspected that Corinne, too, had had about enough of supporting a family.

"Well," I said to Corinne early in December, "only three weeks more."

"Three weeks more?"

"Three more weeks of this and we go back to normal."

"What are you talking about?"

"The experiment was for a year," I said. "And the year will be up in three weeks."

"Michael, we've talked about this before," she said, "and you know there's no way I'm going to go back and be the housewife."

"I'm not asking that," I said. "In fact, I think you should look at it as an experiment. You be the housewife for just a year. I'll pay all the bills and I'll give you a weekly allowance of a hundred dollars."

"Nope."

"I did it. It's only fair."

"If we're talking about real fairness," she said, "then maybe you should do it for the next fifteen years. That's how long I had to do it."

"Maybe we should take a vote," I suggested. "Why don't we elect a mother. That way it'll be up to the family. And I'll vote for you."

178

"That's a great idea," Sean said. "Mom, what's it worth to you if I vote for Dad?"

"I think we ought to look at this seriously for a minute," Corinne said. "You seem to think I mind paying the money. Well, I don't. In fact, I kind of enjoy it. Also, you've been telling us how much you've been enjoying life, well why not keep it going, at least a few more months. The economy is in a bad way now and the business is going well—it would be crazy to upset the apple-cart at this point."

"I'll have to give it some thought."

There was a great deal of truth in what she said. If it was a year ago and I had the decision to make all over again, I wouldn't hesitate for a minute. I would do the same thing. But faced with the decision of whether or not to continue the trade, I was clearly hesitating.

TWENTY-EIGHT

Not only had Corinne been an excellent wife, she was a better husband than I'll ever be. There were no all-night poker games, no carousing with the boys until all hours, no hiding out weekends on the golf course. Moreover, I can't say enough about her as a provider. She paid the bills without a whimper, raised my allowance before I could ask for it. I'm telling you, if more women could find husbands like Corinne, there would be fewer divorces.

While it would be presumptuous of me to judge my success as a homemaker, I do know that it was a decided improvement over recent years. Then, with both of us out chasing a buck, the family had been getting along without a housewife. Meals became less haphazard, shopping was better organized, and some things went more smoothly. I never managed to achieve any competence as a janitor, but I say this with no sense of apology; if I had gotten involved in the cleaning continuum, I would never have had the time for other pursuits. What's more, I never wasted an afternoon watching the soap operas and I didn't open charge accounts at ex-

179

pensive stores and I never once indulged in flirtations with the milkman. In many ways, I was not a bad wife.

Comparing accomplishments over the year, I will concede that Corinne's were the greater. Possibly this is linked to the fact that her challenges were the greater. She had been asked to exercise all her energy and intelligence, while I had regressed to a job that required a good deal more energy than intelligence.

I'm writing these words on the last day of the year, New Year's Eve. Tomorrow will begin a new chapter in our lives and I am just a trifle nervous about it. Starting tomorrow, I'll be paying bills again. How will it go? The economy continues to look bleak; unemployment rises; I have no assurance that there will be room in that jungle for me. It has been months since I've seen any payment for my work—what right do I have to go out and try to be a provider again? What right do I have to ask Corinne to come home again, particularly since there is no guarantee that I can contribute as she has?

I'm not the first housewife to face these questions. I could hold back and be a housewife for another few months, at least until everything seems more settled economically, but the longer I stay away, the harder that return trip is going to seem. I'm not the first housewife who has to take a gamble to go back to work; nor will I be the last.

The closer we've come to understanding the nature of the roles in a marriage, the more important money seems. The freedom of a housewife can be purchased. Once she is in a position to assume some of the financial responsibilities, she can argue most effectively for the sharing of other responsibilities. Unsurprisingly, there is an enormous conspiracy to prevent her from doing just that. The jungle awaiting her ·is a tangle of lower salaries and slower promotions, a solid wall of obstacles and attitudes all seemingly aimed at keeping the servant in the home. The trip is taken one step at a time. A small amount of money purchases a small amount of time; the time can be used for earning more money, for buying more freedom, and so on.

It isn't easy and it doesn't happen overnight. Husbands are not notoriously keen about coming home to frozen dinners and unmade beds. Untended kids can complain as much as neglected husbands. And what is required in these instances is not a soft and loving heart so much as some tough-minded self-interest. It's all a matter of priorities. What is more important, a clean house or a human being free to function? It is entirely possible to have both, but there are times, particularly when the escape is being initiated, when hard choices have to be made.

The Department of Labor reports that there are more than 200,000 men running homes in the United States. However, almost all of these are divorced or widowed or elderly. Warren Farrell, a teacher of sexual politics at American University in Washington, D.C., explained in *Time* magazine why so few men want to be homemakers: "I don't think there are a dozen men in the United States who could survive a year as househusbands. A man would go crazy at home much faster than a woman because he has not learned all his life to play the role of wife."

My feeling is that a person going crazy slowly is not all that better off than a person going crazy fast. I'm not for a minute advocating role reversal; replacing one unpaid servant with another doesn't change the system. The sole benefit of an experiment such as the one we have been going through is that each person will begin to understand the problems of the other; the heart of much real progress rests in one person's ability to put himself in another's shoes.

What we are after is an equal distribution of rights and responsibilities, a classless family.

The old marriage contract, sometimes seen as a trade of male protection for female servitude, never seemed to apply to us. More than sixteen years ago, when Corinne and I drove down to Virginia to elope, Corinne had a sudden change of heart. Why should we bother getting married? What did the vows really mean to us? I argued that it had been a long drive and that we had forked out for the license and gone through the blood test and—well, why not?

She finally agreed—but only reluctantly, only if we would sit down first and write out our own private marriage contract. We wrote the contract on a napkin found in a roadside diner. All in all, there were two dozen clauses covering such things as the guaranteed care and feeding of her old alley cat. One other stipulation provided that we wouldn't let a day pass by without making love.

In time, the alley cat died and so would I have, if we had followed the contract to the letter. That first contract may not have withstood the test of time but at least it was an attempt to live up to our own expectations, not society's. I think now we're ready for another contract, one that will someday undoubtedly seem as out-of-date as our first try.

Drawing up a personal marriage contract is hardly a unique concept today, and one can go to many sources for inspiration. Some feminists advocate the "Marriage Law of the People's Republic of China" which does stress the equality of the sexes within a slightly political framework. ("Husband and wife are in duty bound to love, respect, assist and look after each other, to live in harmony, to engage in productive work, to care for their children and to strive jointly for the welfare of the family and for the building up of the new society.")

Others prefer the contract published by writer Alix Shulman, a marriage agreement that breaks down every responsibility, going so far as to specify which mate takes the temperature and which one calls the doctor. ("This must be worked out equally, since wife now seems to do it all. In any case, wife must be compensated.")

I wanted our agreement to be somewhat more relaxed than that one, somewhat less political than the Chinese model. I have no sense that our contract would apply to any other family but that was not the goal in working it out. It seems to me that our family is in a somewhat enviable position; beginning tomorrow, it will have two breadwinners and two housewives—a sum total of two people, each with the capability of being a husband and each with the experience of being a wife.

The New Year is fast approaching and this may be a little rough. But I would like to have it completed by the time I make my last dinner as a full-time housewife. Lobster thermidor. I wish you could be here. Over the champagne, the family will consider the following agreement.

* * *

GENERAL

The goal is to gain as much freedom as possible—freedom for everyone in the family to grow, to realize potential, to enjoy life to the full. The hope is to have a family that is supportive, each member promoting the well-being of the others. The base is to be one of sharing, an equal division of all responsibilities.

THE EXCHEQUER

It is understood, at the outset, that the money earned by either Corinne or Mike belongs to all members of the family. Our intention is to distribute the financial burden as equitably as possible, thus freeing us all for other pursuits. Although there will be an equal sharing at the beginning, if either of us suffers an economic setback, the other will simply make up the difference. On the other hand, should either of us enjoy a surprising increase in fortune, we will contribute a proportionally larger share to the family exchequer without expectation of compensatory privileges.

Household expenses: All regular household expenses—heat, electricity, gas, mortgage, medical, charity, education, telephone, and so forth—are to be paid from a special joint checking account set up for just this purpose. Corinne and Mike will handle the bookkeeping on alternate months.

The household account: This will be set up on the first of the year by depositing two thousand-dollar checks. The account will be maintained by adding additional thousand-dollar deposits whenever the total on reserve falls below two hundred dollars.

Major purchases: All agreed-upon major purchases for the family—such as furnishing or appliances—are to be paid for in equal shares.

Personal expenses: Individual expenses will be paid from individual accounts. These would include such items as credit-card expenses, personal clothing, car repairs, and, generally, any expenses involving the individual but not the family.

ADULT RESPONSIBILITIES

All the responsibilities of keeping the home and the family are to be divided as fairly and as equitably as possible. To this end, we here initiate the wife-for-a-week program.

The weeks of the year are to be divided equally between Corinne and Mike. On alternate weeks, each is to act as wife and assume the traditional wifely duties for that week. Since this is a non-binding agreement—in fact, the intention is not to bind anyone—we understand there will be exceptions to the pattern, emergencies, and times when days or weeks must be traded.

Food: The wife-for-a-week is to be responsible for shopping and preparing food on that week. The wife-for-a-week will also assume full responsibility for preparing breakfast and lunch for the three children; also for fixing coffee for the husband-for-a-week. Exception: company meals are to be prepared by both Corinne and Mike.

Wife's night out: One night each week, the wife-for-a-week is given an evening away from all wifely duties. This is intended to offer some respite, also to allow each person to follow individual interests without concern to what the rest of the family is doing on that night.

Cleaning: The wife-for-a-week is to see that the house is cleaned thoroughly at least once during the week, either with or without the aid of hired help. The house should be turned over on Monday morning to the new wife-for-a-week in fairly good shape.

Hell Week: Four weeks a year—the first week in January, April, July, and October—will be set aside for doing those jobs that no one wants to do. At the end of Hell Week—and full participation is mandatory—the basement will be clean, the yard will be neat, the trash will be gone, the clothes will be purchased, the sewing will be done and all other agreed-upon tasks will be accomplished. The responsibilities of Hell Week will be equally shared.

CHILDREN'S RESPONSIBILITIES

Servant-for-a-day program: The wife-for-a-week will be assisted by the servant-for-a-day. Each of the three children will assume this role in turn. The primary responsibility for the servant-for-the-day is the kitchen's sanitation-maintenance program.

The servant will be responsible for:

    1. Setting and clearing the table;

2. Doing the dishes;
3. Cleaning the kitchen;
4. Taking out the garbage;
5. Feeding the pets.

SHARED RESPONSIBILITIES

Cleaning of bedrooms: Individuals will be responsible for seeing that bedrooms do not become pigpens.

Laundry: Each individual is responsible for taking care of personal laundry. The entire laundry cycle—washing and drying—is to be done at one time. Clothes are never to be left in the laundry room.

Towels: Each individual has one color of towel and is responsible for all towels of that color. Liam—green; Sean—blue; Siobhan—yellow; Corinne—brown; Mike—red.

Violence: No hitting anyone ever.

Yelling and swearing: No yelling or swearing; especially no yelling or swearing in voices loud enough to be heard by the neighbors.

General Philosophy:
1. Never do anything that bothers, hurts, or interferes with another member of the family.
2. It's a home, not a house, and it should be treated accordingly.
3. Do unto others as you would have them do unto you.

SIGNED: *Mike McGrady*

Corinne McGrady

WITNESSED: *Sean McGrady*

Siobhan McGrady

Liam McGrady

185

233